CASPAR SCHWENCKFELD
ON THE
PERSON AND WORK OF CHRIST

CASPAR SCHWENCKFELD ON THE PERSON AND WORK OF CHRIST

A Study of Schwenckfeldian Theology at its Core

BY

PAUL L. MAIER

Wipf & Stock
PUBLISHERS
Eugene, Oregon

Wipf and Stock Publishers
199 W 8th Ave, Suite 3
Eugene, OR 97401

Caspar Schwenckfeld on the Person and Work of Christ
A Study of Schwenckfeldian Theology at Its Core
By Maier, Paul L.
Copyright©1959 by Maier, Paul L.
ISBN: 1-59244-754-6
Publication date 7/6/2004
Previously published by Royal VanGorcum, Ltd., 1959

ERRATA

Page

14, l. 28: "Schw." for "Schw,"
34, l. 17: omit comma
36, l. 2: "state" for "sate"
52, l. 26: "1" before footnote
59, l. 44: "Virgin" for "Vrigin"
88, l. 30: "the" for "he"
89, l. 16: hyphenate "mysticallyaccented"
96, l. 36: "geschaffenen" for "geschaffen"
98, l. 20: "," for " ' "
105, l. 17: "placed" for "places"

PREFACE

A major concern in contemporary Reformation research has been an exploration of the variety of *Nebenströmungen* or side-currents issuing from the great religious upheaval. While Luther, Zwingli, Calvin, and other reformers will never be diverted from the main stream of scholarly concern with the sixteenth century, much of the present interest in the Reformation has, in fact, become centered in movements parallel to the orthodox Protestant traditions deriving from this time. Anabaptists, Spiritualists, mystics, and Anti-Trinitarians – once obscure religionists blanketed by the haze of four centuries – are now finding their place in the Reformation sun.

Of the mystically speculative writers within these movements, Caspar Schwenckfeld and Sebastian Frank were by far the most influential. The leading theologian and certainly the most prolific writer among the Spiritualists was the remarkable Schwenckfeld. Cordially blessed or blamed by contemporaries, his teachings have long deserved objective and detailed research.

This study comprises both a review of the more significant aspects of Schwenckfeld's theology, particularly his points of dissent with other reformers, as well as an exposition of the core of Schwenckfeldian – as of all Christian – theology: the doctrine of the person and work of Christ. It is hoped that this monograph will provide a convenient path into the center of Schwenckfeld's thought, which may to some extent obviate the need of taking in hand the seventeen tomes of the *Corpus Schwenckfeldianorum*. – In this connection we salute the Schwenkfelders, some two thousand spiritual descendants of the Silesian theologian now living predominantly in Pennsylvania, who brought out the massive *Corpus*. – The author's ultimate concern is that this body of source material, together with such studies as his own, may fill a serious gap in the history of the Reformation Era.

I am particularly indebted to the following for their gracious assistance: Prof. George Hunston Williams of Harvard Divinity School, for having pointed out the necessity of further investigation into Schwenckfeld's theology; Prof. Heinrich Bornkamm of the University of Heidelberg, who provided helpful suggestions in the early stages of this research; Selina Gerhard Schultz, Associate and Managing Editor of the *Corpus Schwenckfeldianorum* and author of the biography *Caspar Schwenckfeld von Ossig*, who kindly supplied information and materials; and especially Dr. Ernst Staehelin, Professor of Church History at the University of Basel, whose guidance and criticism were greatly valued in the preparation of this monograph. Originally a dissertation submitted for the degree of Doctor of Philosophy at the University of Basel, this study necessarily benefited from the atmosphere generated by such of my other teachers as Profs. Oscar Cullmann, Karl Barth, and Denis van Berchem.

My appreciation is also extended to the head librarians of the Universities of Basel and Heidelberg, the British Museum, and the Schwenckfelder Library, Pennsburg, Pennsylvania; to the Department of State, Washington, D.C., for the award of a United States Government Grant under the Fulbright Act, through which this research was partially completed; to the Lutheran World Federation, Geneva, for having provided a special study grant; and to Prof. Julius Schweizer of the University of Basel, James Wagner, and my brother, Rev. Walter A. Maier, Jr., for having read the manuscript.

Final gratitude is due my parents, to whom I also dedicate this volume as a token of my esteem.

Festival of the Reformation, 1958   PAUL L. MAIER

TABLE OF CONTENTS

PREFACE v
CHAPTER I.   INTRODUCTION 1

PART I
SURVEY OF SCHWENCKFELD'S DOMINANT THEOLOGICAL CONCERNS

CHAPTER II.   ETHICS 9
CHAPTER III. MEDIATING THEOLOGY 12
CHAPTER IV.   THE SACRAMENTS 15
CHAPTER V.   DOCTRINE OF THE WORD 26

PART II
THE CHRISTOLOGICAL FOCUS

CHAPTER VI   DERIVATION OF SCHWENCKFELD'S DOCTRINE OF THE PERSON AND WORK OF CHRIST . . . 33
CHAPTER VII. ANTHROPOLOGICAL PRESUPPOSITIONS. . . . 41

PART III
EXPOSITION OF SCHWENCKFELDIAN CHRISTOLOGY AND SOTERIOLOGY

CHAPTER VIII. THE PRE-EXISTENT WORD 47
CHAPTER IX.   CHRIST IN THE STATE OF HUMILIATION . . . 52
CHAPTER X.   CHRIST IN THE STATE OF EXALTATION . . . 71
CHAPTER XI.   PARTICIPATION IN CHRIST 83

CHAPTER XII. CONCLUSION 106

BIBLIOGRAPHY 111

CHAPTER I

INTRODUCTION

As scholarship continues to unfold the history of the Reformation Era, the name of Caspar Schwenckfeld (1489-1561) occurs with ever greater frequency in many different areas of the theology and life of that age. We find the nobleman and lay reformer from Ossig in Silesia [1] pleading with Luther, debating with Melanchthon, disputing with Bucer, being published by Zwingli, and arguing with such Anabaptists as Hoffman and Marbeck. His friends and foes included dozens of other prominent names in the sixteenth century. It is not an exaggeration to claim that Caspar Schwenckfeld was one of the most prolific writers and influential theologians of his day to arise outside the orthodox Protestant traditions. Strangely, however, we know more about the theologies of many who wrote less than did Schwenckfeld and whose writings are less readily available. Any investigation of his doctrines, therefore, needs apology only for its tardiness.

This study should begin by emphasizing that Schwenckfeld was not a systematician, for his ultimate interests were religious and ethical rather than speculative and theological (V, 102).[2] It was in the practical task of applying the Protestant gospel in Silesia, however, that Schwenckfeld forged his own theological weapons to combat what he deemed the ethical deficiencies of the Reformation, broke with Wittenberg, and was forced willy-nilly into the theological arena from which he never withdrew. Although theologizing remained something

---

[1] For biographical details, see the first complete life of Schwenckfeld by Selina Gerhard Schultz, *Caspar Schwenckfeld von Ossig* (Norristown, Pennsylvania, 1947). Franz Hoffmann, *Caspar Schwenckfelds Leben und Lehren*, Erster Teil (Berlin, 1897), is accurate to the year 1524. O. Hampe, *Zur Biographie Kaspars v. Schwenckfeld* (Jauer, 1882), is also limited, but does extend to 1539. Oswald Kadelbach, *Ausfuhrliche Geschichte Kaspar v. Schwenckfelds und der Schwenkfelder in Schlesien, der Ober-Lausitz und Amerika* (Lauban, 1860), tells us more about the Schwenckfelders than Schwenckfeld. Other works give only such a *Lebenslauf* as can be found in the standard sets of reference.

[2] Here and in each such documentation hereafter, the Roman numeral signifies the volume number in the *Corpus Schwenckfeldianorum*, and the Arabic numerals the page or pages. Three or more such references are footnoted.

of an *opus alienum* for the Silesian reformer, his production was enormous. The same Philip Melanchthon who taunted Schwenckfeld for not having drawn up a system (XIII, 976, 1001) was clearly astonished at the profusion of his letters and theological treatises, which, he concluded, only a "hundred-hander" (*centimanus*) could have written.[1] To most contemporary dogmaticians, indeed, Schwenckfdeld's writings seemed little more than a "perverse accumulation of the strangest idiosyncrasies," as Dorner has phrased it,[2] and the judgment of succeeding generations was not much kinder. Although even today the purist will find something less than precision in his treatises, there are, nevertheless, elements of consistency and clarity in what – by generous definition – may be termed Schwenckfeld's "theological system." This "system," to be sure, is not articulated in concise definitions or scholastic formulations; it was intended chiefly for his friends and followers, a theologically literate laity. Schwenckfeld, however, never recoiled from debate with the ranking theologians of his day and often enough proved himself more than a match for many of them.

The central concentration in Schwenckfeld's theology is neither his concept of the Eucharist, nor the Church,[3] nor "Word and Spirit," [4] but the doctrines concerning the person and work of Christ. Christological and soteriological themes clearly bulk largest in the some fifteen thousand pages of the latest critical edition of his works,[5] and this emphasis is reflected in the name which Schwenckfeld chose for his followers: "Confessors of the Glory of Christ" rather than "Schwenkfeldians" (XIII, 161-63). Matching the magnitude of his writings, however, is the difficulty involved in attempting precisely to understand the Silesian reformer in this area of his greatest religious sensitivity and productivity. Nowhere is Schwenckfeld more apparently paradoxical, incomprehensible, unsystematic, yet original, involved, and crusading than in his christological doctrines. Here are

[1] *Corpus Reformatorum* (hereafter *CR*), ed. by K. G. Bretschneider *et al.*, 1834 ff., VIII, 740.

[2] J. A. Dorner, *Entwicklungsgeschichte der Lehre von der Person Christi*, Zweiter Theil (Berlin, 1853), p. 624.

[3] *Sic* Walther Kohler, who, in his critique of Ecke's book (*vide infra*) in *Theologische Literaturzeitung*, 1913, p. 211, states: "Im Kirchenideal liegt der Schwerpunkt der Schwenckfeldischen Gedankenwelt."

[4] *Sic* Richard H. Grützmacher, *Wort und Geist* (Leipzig, 1902), p. 159, who asserts. "... wirklich die Frage nach dem Verhältnis von Wort und Geist im Mittelpunkte seiner Theologie steht." Cf. also the article by Grutzmacher, "Schwenckfeld," *Realencyklopädie für protestantische Theologie und Kirche*, Dritte Aufl., XVIII (1906), 76, where the same opinion is voiced.

[5] The *Corpus Schwenckfeldianorum* (hereafter *CS*), fifteen volumes (Leipzig, 1907-1939), includes Schw.'s writings from 1521 to 1557. Volumes XVI and XVII are in process of publication.

most of the more controversial theologoumena and the *nova* in his theology, and here is where Schwenckfeld was most vulnerable, misunderstood, and attacked both in his own time and subsequently. Perhaps for this reason a longer systematic study of his doctrine of Christ has thus far largely been neglected. Not a few of the older historians of dogma have seconded the suggestion of the otherwise objective C. A. Salig that Schwenckfeld would have done better had he avoided a detailed Christology and contented himself merely with the production of morally edifying literature instead.[1] Even today, one of the latest monographs on Schwenckfeld despairs of any success in bringing his Christology to logical clarity and largely avoids the subject.[2] Others, perhaps, have awaited the appearance of the entire *Corpus Schwenckfeldianorum* before examining the interpretation of Christ's person and work set forth therein.

Several important studies of Schwenckfeld's doctrine of Christ have, however, appeared, all since the beginning of the nineteenth century. While his Christology had been investigated before this time, the research was usually compromised by the same prejudice which colored most discussions of Schwenckfeld until the last century. Or, where he was accorded an impartial appraisal, as in Arnold [3] and Salig,[4] Christology was largely ignored. Typical of this earlier approach is G. J. Planck,[5] who made a comparatively larger study of Schwenckfeldian Christology, but patterned his work on the clauses in the *Formula Concordiae* which condemned the reformer's theology! Although some of his critique is justified, Schwenckfeld receives the same *"Schwärmer"* appraisal usually accorded him in the lists of the orthodox heresiologists [6]

Ferdinand Christian Baur apparently stimulated a renaissance in Schwenckfeld research. Touching on the reformer's soteriology in 1838,[7] he discussed certain aspects of his Christology three years later,[8] and again in 1848.[9] Not always with entire objectivity, Baur stresses the speculative and mystical

---

[1] Christian August Salig, *Vollstandige Historie der Augspurgischen Confession und derselben Apologie zugethanen Kirchen* (Halle, 1735), Dritter Theil, pp. 1017 f.

[2] Gottfried Maron, *Individualismus und Gemeinschaft bei Caspar v. Schwenckfeld* (Unpublished dissertation, University of Gottingen, 1956), p. 47.

[3] Gottfried Arnold, *Unpartheyische Kirchen- und Ketzerhistorien* (Schaffhausen, 1740), Bd. I, Th. II, Buch XVI, pp. 1246-99.

[4] Salig, *op. cit.*, pp. 950-1092.

[5] *Geschichte der Entstehung, der Veranderungen, und der Bildung unseres protestantischen Lehrbegriffs* (Leipzig, 1798), Funften Bandes erster Theil, pp. 75-250.

[6] Cf., e.g., Conrad Schlusselburg, "De Stenckfeldistis," *Catalogus haereticorum* (Frankfurt, 1599), X; also Johann Wigand, *De Schwengfeldismo. Dogmata et argumenta"* (Lipsiae, 1587).

[7] *Die christliche Lehre von der Versohnung in ihrer geschichtlichen Entwicklung* (Tubingen, 1838), pp. 459-63.

[8] *Die christliche Lehre von der Dreieinigkeit und Menschwerdung Gottes in ihrer geschichtlichen Entwicklung* (Tubingen, 1841-43), Dritter Theil, pp. 219-56.

[9] "Zur Geschichte der protestantischen Mystik," *Theologische Jahrbucher*, VII (1848), 502-28.

depths of the Schwenckfeldian system, but does provide us with a penetrating evaluation. In 1847 appeared the first – and since then, the last – systematic inquiry into Schwenckfeldian Christology and soteriology, G. L. Hahn's *Schwenckfeldii Sententia de Christi Persona et Opere Exposita*.[1] Hahn's research is praiseworthy and accurate, although somewhat abbreviated. The object of this study is not so much a discussion with Hahn, as an enlargement and supplementation of the same theme. Moreover, with the appearance of the *Corpus Schwenckfeldianorum*, a greater quantity of source material is accessible to the contemporary researcher than could conveniently have been available to Hahn. H. W. Erbkam's commendable discussion in 1848,[2] which is half-biographical and half-theological, does not intend a detailed representation of Schwenckfeld's christological doctrines, but rather centers on his relationship to mysticism in general. Schwenckfeldian Christology and soteriology receive excellent, if necessarily limited, treatment by J. A. Dorner in his two studies of 1853[3] and 1867.[4]

In this century appeared F. W. Loetscher's monograph on Schwenckfeld's doctrine of the Eucharist.[5] The discussion, however, is not limited to the reformer's concept of the sacraments, but provides penetrating insights into, and criticism of, his soteriology as well. T. Sippell's review[6] of K. Ecke's research into Schwenckfeld's concept of the church[7] also contains a perceptive summary of the major themes in his doctrine of Christ. In 1922 Emanuel Hirsch[8] made an acute study of the genetics of certain Schwenckfeldian doctrines, including Christology. Finally, Wach in 1946,[9] Koyré in 1950,[10] and Schoeps in 1951[11] touched on the christological core of Schwenckfeld's theology. Schoeps' monograph contains discerning passages, but also statements which require some modification.[12]

[1] Georgius Ludovicus Hahn, *Schwenckfeldii Sententia de Christi Persona et Opere Exposita. Commentatio Historico-Theologica* (Vratislaviae, MDCCCXLVII).

[2] *Geschichte der protestantischen Sekten im Zeitalter der Reformation* (Hamburg und Gotha, 1848), pp. 357-475.

[3] *Op. cit.*, pp. 575-81, 624-36.

[4] *Geschichte der protestantischen Theologie* (Munchen, 1867), pp. 176-82.

[5] Frederick William Loetscher, "Schwenckfeld's Participation in the Eucharistic Controversy of the Sixteenth Century," *The Princeton Theological Review*, IV (July, 1906), 352-86, and (Oct., 1906), 454-500.

[6] Theodor Sippell, "Caspar Schwenckfeld," *Die Christliche Welt*, XXV (1911), 865-71, 897-900, 925-27, 955-57, 963-66.

[7] Karl Ecke, *Schwenckfeld, Luther und der Gedanke einer apostolischen Reformation* (Berlin, 1911).

[8] "Zum Verstandnis Schwenckfelds," *Festgabe von Fachgenossen und Freunden Karl Muller* (Tubingen, 1922), pp. 145-70.

[9] Joachim Wach, "Caspar Schwenckfeld, A Pupil and a Teacher in the School of Christ," *The Journal of Religion*, XXVI (1946), 1-29.

[10] Alexandre Koyré, *Mystiques, Spirituels, Alchimistes du XVIe siècle allemand* (Paris, 1955).

[11] Hans Joachim Schoeps, "Vom Himmlischen Fleisch Christi," *Sammlung Gemeinverständlicher Vorträge und Schriften aus dem Gebiet der Theologie und Religionsgeschichte*, 195/196 (Tubingen, 1951), pp. 25-36.

[12] This summary is not intended as a synopsis of general research on Schwenckfeld, but only of that literature which is directly concerned with his Christology and soteriology.

This study will place more emphasis upon an objective presentation of Schwenckfeld's doctrine of the person and work of Christ than on an extended criticism of the same. It is unfortunate that much of Schwenckfeld research has rather been characterized by the inverse approach. In the zeal to classify the lay theologian by dogmatic relegation to some pattern or corner in the history of dogma rather than to make a comprehensive study of his writings, too often the researcher and not Schwenckfeld has spoken. Begun with the suspicion that Schwenckfeld's christological doctrines have a definite coherence and hardly constitute a speculative cul-de-sac, this study will attempt to systematize the unsystematic, but not, certainly, at the cost of ignoring evident inconsistencies.

PART I

SURVEY OF SCHWENCKFELD'S DOMINANT THEOLOGICAL CONCERNS

CHAPTER II

ETHICS

Before discussing Christology and soteriology in detail, a brief review of Schwenckfeld's other theological interests is indicated both by way of introduction to our theme, and also because his doctrines of the person and work of Christ developed historically out of related prior concerns.

As previously noted, Schwenckfeld's guiding motivation lay in the area of practical Christianity. At first championing Luther and the cause of the Reformation in his native Silesia (XIV, 802), Schwenckfeld soon questioned the moral efficacy of Wittenberg's gospel and concluded that doctrines such as justification *sola fide*, bondage of the will, "uselessness" of works, and divine predestination were being understood by the common people in an external and libertine sense.[1] This situation, compounded by his offense at the quartering of Christ's church into Roman Catholic, Lutheran, Zwinglian, and Anabaptist divisions, led Schwenckfeld to institute what he termed the "Reformation of the Middle Way." [2] This endeavor was to emphasize both a warm, personal, practical Christianity, which clearly anticipated and influenced Pietism,[3] and a mediating theology.

To implement the practical aspects of his program, Schwenckfeld authored a steady stream of letters, tracts, and treatises for the edification of his readers. Even if he did not produce a systematic ethics – and that discipline had not yet been isolated as such – his practical theology with its emphasis on regeneration and the new man,[4]

[1] Cf. Schw.'s first important treatise, "Ermanung Des misszbrauchs Etzlicher furnemstenn Artickell des Euangelij/ auss welcher unverstant der gemein man in fleischliche freyheit und irrug gefuret wirt" (1524), II, 28 ff. Other passages which bewail ethical deficiencies of the Reformation include. II, 218, 330, 652 ff.; VIII, 440; X, 23. In II, 368 the situation is described as "ihe lenger, ihe erger." XIV, 855 ff. is based in part upon the treatise cited above. Schw. was thus concerned with this problem throughout his career.

[2] II, 62 is the first occurrence of this phrase, after which it is found *passim*.

[3] Cf. Valentin Ernst Loescher, *Dissertatio de Schvengfeldismo in Pietismo renato* (Wittenberger Disputation, XI (Okt., 1708); also Ecke, *op. cit.*, pp. 285-95; and Hirsch, *op. cit.*, p. 169.

[4] See "Von dreierlai Leben der menschen" (1546), IX, 828 ff., Schw.'s most important ethical treatise.

education of the conscience,[1] patience under the cross,[2] and Christian prayer,[3] aimed at a reformation of life as well as doctrine. Himself a man of unassailable character and clear conscience,[4] Schwenckfeld faced the vituperative abuse directed at him through much of his life with exemplary composure.

Occasionally, indeed, he betrayed puritanical tendencies, especially in his emphasis on restricted *ecclesiolae* or conventicles of the truly regenerate who, in contrast to the masses of nominal Christians, were alone worthy to receive the sacraments, and among whom only a truly consecrated ministry could render any effective service.[5] In fact, some of Schwenckfeld's phraseology would appear to classify him as the Novatian of the Reformation Era, e.g.: "They [Lutheran preachers] ...wish to bring more people to heaven than God wants there" (IV, 834; V, 132). Schwenckfeld, however, was never a theological perfectionist, as incorrectly charged in the *Formula Concordiae*,[6] and his consistent exponency of full religious tolerance also provided a marked contrast to the attitudes of some of his contemporaries.[7] Nor was he the rank moralist who might insist, "One should not know much, but only live piously" (XII, 390). For true Christian piety could proceed only from "the knowledge of God and the understanding of Christ" (III, 385 ff.). Similarly, faith was never blind or uninformed. Ignorance of the mysteries apprehended by faith implied disqualification from those mysteries (III, 178). Hence Schwenckfeld's aversion to what he considered the misunderstanding and abysmal spiritual ignorance of the Christians of his day, particularly in the doctrines of the Lord's Supper, Word and sacrament in general, and especially

---

[1] See esp. "Vom guten und bosen gewissen" (1529), III, 442 ff.

[2] Schw. brought out an edition of the *Imitatio Christi* in 1531, IV, 265 ff. See also "Catechismus Vom Worte des Creutzes" (1545), IX, 451 ff.; and "Vonn der himlischen artzney des waren artzets Christi" (1545), IX, 518 ff.

[3] See "Vom Gebeet" (1547), X, 1007 ff. Cf. V, 830 ff.

[4] Even his enemies admitted this. Wach, *op. cit.*, 1, does not exaggerate in asserting "There can be no doubt that Caspar Schwenckfeld von Ossig is one of the worthiest and most attractive figures in the era of the Reformation — nay, in the history of Christianity."

[5] II, 658, III, 145 ff.; IV, 805; esp. IX, 169.

[6] IV, 723, *et passim*. Cf. "Errores Schwenckfeldianorum," *Formula Concordiae*, Solida Declaratio XII, v; Epitome XII, vi.

[7] See esp. Schw.'s letters to Leo Jud, pastor in Zurich, on Christian liberty, IV, Doc. CXLI and CXLIII; also V, 293 ff.; X, 551, and "Ain Bedencken Von der Freiheit des Glaubens," to be published as Doc. MCLIX in XVI. Cf. Johannes Kuhn, *Toleranz und Offenbarung* (Leipzig, 1923), pp. 140-56

Christology-soteriology.[1] The "Reformation of the Middle Way" would therefore involve not only a program of education and moral enlightenment, but also a mediating theology primarily as a corrective to the Lutheran gospel, which, according to Schwenckfeld and his Silesian associates, had little empirical effect upon the commonality.

[1] II, 658; VIII, 440, *et passim.*

CHAPTER III

A MEDIATING THEOLOGY

Middle Way theology placed its mean between different extremes, depending upon the particular doctrine or theologoumenon in question. In the faith-works tension, Schwenckfeld assumed a position between Roman Catholicism, with a gospel which he recognized as corrupted but stressing a rigid morality,[1] and Lutheranism, which had the true gospel but, in his estimation, no strong ethical emphasis.[2] The Middle Way accented both faith and works in Schwenckfeld's synthesis, a form of essential justification. In the controversy over free will, Schwenckfeld took his stand between Luther and Erasmus, asserting that in the old man the will is enslaved, but in the new it is free. The doctrine of predestination he accepted and quoted against synergists, but he avoided the negative aspects of the dogma, chided the Swiss for

---

[1] Indeed, Schw. went so far as to say that he would have joined the Roman Catholic church had only freedom of conscience been allowed him, III, 106. This passage, however, is very exceptional and should not be isolated as representative of Schw.'s attitude toward Rome. Not a few modern histories of dogma make this mistake. Schw. remained a true Protestant and usually voiced opinions directly opposed to the above citation. Cf., e.g., "SECESSVS EX ROMANA ECCLESIA, ET CVR NON EAM HABEAMVS PRO Ecclesia Christi," VII, 368 f., in which Schw. listed thirty-six reasons. Cf. also XII, 641, where he drew up a list of twenty points of doctrine which he held in common with the Lutherans.

[2] Schw. seems to have overlooked the strong ethical implications in Luther's doctrine. He was rather offended by the very failure in practice about which Luther himself complained. Despite subsequent difficulties with him, however, Schw. remained lastingly indebted to Luther for repristinating the gospel, cf. II, 83; IV, 29 ff.; esp. VIII, 689, and XII, 641.

A separate, detailed study of the precise influence of Luther upon Schw. is a *desideratum*. Hirsch, *op. cit.*, makes a sagacious start at tracing the young Schw.'s indebtedness to Luther, which he demonstrates as substantial. Ecke stresses the positive relationship to such an extent that we are left with a near-caricature of Schw. as "der schlesische Lutheraner," *op. cit.*, p. 37, 88, or "genuiner Lutheraner," p. 45.

In explaining his own progressive separation from Wittenberg, Schw. constantly maintained that the young Luther shared his views on the nature of Word and sacrament, the immediacy of the inner Word, and the dispensability of external sacraments. That Luther's theology before the outbreak of the Wittenberg disturbances in 1521-22 did contain some subjective elements which contrasted with his subsequent objectivity on the doctrines of Word and sacrament is, of course, a matter of common knowledge.

making it central in their system, and repudiated a double election.[1] In the Eucharistic controversy, Middle Way theology rejected both Luther's interpretation and Zwingli's *significat*, teaching instead a true presence of Christ, but unattached to the elements. As to the relationship between Word and Spirit, Schwenckfeld denied the Lutheran means of grace, yet also disavowed the enthusiasm of the Anabaptists. Even the Christology of the Silesians attempted to chart a course in the narrows between the Nestorian and Eutychian extremes in Reformation theology, although it nearly shoaled on the latter.

Already distressed at the schism which had produced four parties in Christendom, Schwenckfeld had no intention of creating a fifth with his mediating theology. Once he and his associates had arrived at their characteristic tenets, however, they maintained them with an uncompromising consistency. Inevitably, Schwenckfeldianism took its place among the sects rather than achieving its aim of constituting the golden mean in Christendom.

The guiding principle of Schwenckfeld's theology, his *"Primum Theologiae Principium,"* was *"die Erkenntnis Christi,"* the genuine knowledge of Christ and the true faith apprehending this knowledge.[2] In fact, he summarized his entire theology as *"Erkenntnis Christi"* (XIII, 985), and even amended the Reformation formula to include the phrase: "Justification derives from the *knowledge of Christ* through faith" (X, 707; cf. XII, 814). This knowledge, the one necessary thing on earth (VII, 379), the true foundation of the church (XI, 852) and eternal life (IV, 216), transcends any human knowledge acquired through the senses. It must come directly from God himself through the divine revelation of the Holy Spirit, and not by the agency of any external, earthly, or creaturely means, including the Holy Scriptures (III, 31, *et passim*). Indeed, Jesus Christ is himself the only "Means of Grace" or Mediator, and he mediates himself internally.[3]

---

[1] Cf. esp. IV, 89 ff. Of the deterministic excesses of the doctrine, Schw. asserted that no more pernicious teaching had ever entered Christendom. Such an absolute predestination was "ein philosophisch haidnisch dogma," IV, 93. Koyre, *op. cit.*, p. 9, is mistaken in asserting: "Il l'accepte [la doctrine de prédestination] dans toute sa riguer. La prédestination est absolue." Again, predestination is not, as Grutzmacher, *op. cit.*, p. 160, would have it, the ultimate reason for Schw.'s stressing the immediacy of Christ and the believer. For the practical Christian life, in Schw.'s estimation, an absolute view of the doctrine was too unethical, too impractical, and really invaded the hidden will of God. The Christian was rather to seek his salvation in Christ, the revealed Will of God, XII, 910 ff.

[2] VIII, 663; cf. also II, 578; III, 386; IV, 216, 679; VII, 379; VIII, 31, *et passim*.

[3] III, 509: "Christus unicus mediator noster est, per quem nobis bona celestia conferantur. Nulla alioqui cooperatio rerum celestium ad elementa istius mundi." Cf. IV, 37; XIII, 83.

The immediacy of Christ and the Christian is a fundamental theological postulate which Schwenckfeld shared with the spiritualistic left wing of the Reformation. It presupposes, in his theology, an axiomatic cosmological, ontological, philosophical, and psychological dualism which dichotomizes the universe into the internal and external, the spiritual and material, the divine and creaturely. This fundamental distinction, which Schwenckfeld probably learned from Tauler and a Neo-Platonism filtered through patristic writings,[1] can be observed in nearly every doctrine with which he concerned himself. Thus Schwenckfeld speaks of an internal and external food and drink in the Lord's Supper, two washings and waters in baptism, an inner and outer Word of God, two kinds of ministry, faith, justification, righteousness, revelation, birth, children, men, teaching, life – in fine, a twofold essence of all things.[2] It cannot be overemphasized how Schwenckfeld's entire theology, particularly his anthropology, Christology, and his doctrines of Word and sacrament are indelibly stamped with this dichotomy and its implications. Since the inner and the spiritual can affect only something else within the spiritual realm, and the outer and the material are limited to the physical, these two orders or spheres are independent of each other, and there is no necessary correlation between them. Accordingly, Schwenckfeld would tolerate no intermixture between the spiritual and the physical, as if the one enlisted or were conferred through the other, which he termed the cardinal error in the Lutheran doctrine of the means of grace.

[1] The influence of the fathers and esp. Tauler on the origins of Schw.'s theology will be discussed *infra*.

[2] Cf. esp. II, 454. This dichotomy is also illustrated in II, 307, 354 ff., 404, 468, 485; III, 113. 176; IV, 549; V, 66-69; VIII, 188; IX, 113; X, 292. For schematic diagrams which Schw, drew to illustrate the theological implications of this dichotomy, see XV, 12-15.

CHAPTER IV

THE SACRAMENTS

With these presuppositions in mind, let us briefly examine Schwenckfeld's understanding of a means of grace and his doctrines of sacrament and Word. Since such divine entities as grace, faith, the Holy Spirit, or Christ are spiritual in essence, they must be communicated to the believer by God without benefit of any material means and received by the spiritual part of man through an "inner hearing."[1] This reception can take place instantaneously, effecting a conversion apart from any human ministry (II, 505; III, 515). In communicating Christ and his grace, the Holy Ghost is attached neither to "time, apostle, Scripture, preaching, or reading" (VII, 122 f.). Eminently free, the Spirit "'spirits' [*geistet*] where, when, and to what extent he wishes" (VII, 122).

Schwenckfeld, however, did not arrive at the extremes of radical spiritualism to which such expressions would theoretically lead. In practice he was not an enthusiast or *Schwärmer*, and, although he is often classed with them, Schwenckfeld acknowledged no fellowship in "faith, teaching, or life" with Sebastian Franck or Hans Bünderlin, and censured them for suspending externals in their concern with the inner Word and Spirit (VII, 152). In fact, one of Schwenckfeld's major objections to the Anabaptists was their wholesale enthusiastic position.[2]

---

[1] II, 504 ff., 686 ff. For the severest Silesian condemnation of any orthodox means of grace, see esp. "Von der gnaden Gottes" (1528), authored by Schw.'s associate, Valentine Crautwald, and edited by Schw., III, 85 ff. Schw.'s classical expression in this regard is his foundation treatise, "De Cursu Verbi Dei" (1527), II, 581 ff. Cf. also III, 877 ff., 896, 928; XII, 814, *et passim*.

[2] Schw.'s relations with the Anabaptists follow a course of progressive deterioration. Their basic insistence on rebaptism he regarded as unwarranted, but at first he did admire their religious zeal and pleaded toleration in their behalf, III, 831 f., IV, 833. In attempting to carry on discussions with Anabaptist leaders, however, Schw. was rebuffed and subsequently attacked, III, 79. Later in life he grew increasingly critical of their movement and charged

Later in life he summarized what he considered the two erring doctrinal extremes so far as the course of divine grace was concerned:

> First are the Lutherans, who attach to their ministry far too much, indeed, what it behooves Christ alone to confer; who direct the people to seek salvation from themselves and their preached word and sacrament. They permit their hearers to rely solely on what they preach or dictate to them, and call it God's word.... They point them to Scriptural texts, but not, through a penitent life, heavenward to Christ, the reigning King.
>
> . . . .
>
> The others, however, who indiscriminately reject entirely the ministry of the external word; who have no regard for, nor read, Holy Scriptures, nor perceive God's talents in men; who wish to learn only from God and despise his servants who teach correctly as well as God's gracious gifts in them – these transgress on the left side and scorn not men, but Christ himself, who said of his dear apostles, indeed, of all those in whom he has placed his word in their heart and mouth and who teach in his grace, "Whoever hears you hears me, and whoever rejects you rejects me, etc.," Luke 10. It happens also to some out of sheer pride and selfishness, as if they stood so high in the Spirit and in God's graces that he had daily conversation with them, so that they now no longer required the service or doctrine of any man (XII, 129).

Although he was searching for a middle ground between Wittenberg and the enthusiasts, Schwenckfeld found in the Lutheran means of grace the more formidable doctrinal entrenchment and the greater error. Accordingly, much of his energy was directed against Wittenberg, and his stand necessarily inclined to the theological left. But full-blown *Schwärmer* he could not be, even according to the presuppositions of his system. For besides the spiritual-internal-divine order there was also the material-external-creaturely; and if man himself is so divided, and his total self to be affected by God's activity, then the outer man must also be influenced in some manner. Such externals, therefore, as preaching, the ministry, and the administration of the sacraments do have a justified existence, however subordinate, in Schwenckfeld's system.

This is best illustrated by his doctrine of the sacraments. Schwenckfeld did not jettison the term "sacrament," but even defended its use against those who regarded the sacraments as mere signs rather than

---

them with legalism, intolerance, and ignorance. Cf. VIII, 865-68, where he upbraids them in strong language. Ludwig Keller, *Die Reformation und die älteren Reformparteien* (Leipzig, 1885), p. 462, incorrectly categorizes Schw. with Franck as a foremost representative of the "freien Taufer." For the latest summary of Schw.'s controversy with the Anabaptists, see Torsten Bergsten, "Pilgram Marbeck und seine Auseinandersetzung mit Casper Schwenckfeld," *Kyrkohistorisk Årsskrift* (1957-58) Uppsala, 1958, 39-135.

the mysteries of God.[1] His own brief definition reads: *Sacramenta constant ex visibili signo et invisibili gratia, sed vnum non est in reliquo neque datur per reliquum* (III, 510). Indeed, Schwenckfeld regarded no sacrament as complete before God unless both the spiritual grace and material sign were present, as commanded by Christ himself (IV, 116, 122). This did not, however, imply that the inner grace and outer sign were mutually bound to one another. While the spiritual benefits could be mediated independently of the external observance, the outer celebration capitulated its very *raison d'être* if a parallel or prior communication of grace did not take place within the spiritual realm (V, 170). Nowhere did Schwenckfeld give clearer or more positive expression to his doctrine of the sacraments than in the following citation from the year 1531:

> Neither Christ, nor his grace, nor the Spirit is bound to the use of the sacraments, nor attached to any external thing. Through Christ, God effects such a mystery freely in the Spirit where and when he finds the soul prepared through faith that it desires his grace and activity, be it immediately before the use of the sacrament, in the use, after the use, without the use, and with the use. Just as he works before the sermon, in the sermon, without the sermon, and with the sermon, independently in divine spiritual freedom.... *Should such occur apart from the use of the sacraments, it must nevertheless take place to a greater degree and more powerfully where the institution of Christ is followed also externally and practiced in the obedience of faith with correct understanding and use.* Where these two parts – the correct understanding and use – do not obtain, then it is better to omit [the sacraments] and apprehend the grace of God in other ways, so that the individual does not receive death, punishment, and condemnation where he supposed he would find life and salvation, as was the case in Corinth [2]

When correctly observed, therefore, the external sacraments fulfilled a distinct positive function in pointing the outer man to Christ, and thus *serving toward* the grace and salvation which they could not, however, mediate.[3] For this reason Schwenckfeld did not reject even such externals as religious painting and sculpture (XI, 155).

---

[1] III, 427; IV, 146-48. Cf., however, IX, 687, where Schw. does question the word "sacrament" for the first time, yet approves its usage primarily in view of ecclesiastical tradition.

[2] IV, 132 f. (italics mine). It should, however, be remembered that Schw. never again expressed himself so favorably on the sacraments.

[3] III, 879. Schw.'s view of the sacraments, thus, somewhat exceeds the negative estimate he is often credited with possessing. E.g., Eduard Anders, *Geschichte der evangelischen Kirche Schlesiens* (Breslau, 1886), p. 59, asserts that Schw. regarded baptism and the Lord's Supper as "leere Ceremonien."

The Lord's Supper

Schwenckfeld's understanding of the Eucharist [1] was the immediate occasion of his formal break with Luther and remained a fundamental *casus belli* with Wittenberg throughout his life. Indeed, the voluminous writings on this doctrine in the *Corpus Schwenckfeldianorum* are second in quantity only to the treatises on the person and work of Christ.

At first sharing Luther's view on the real presence,[2] Schwenckfeld, in 1525, became concerned about the case of Judas, who, he reasoned, could never have betrayed his Lord had he truly partaken of the essential body and blood of Christ in the Supper; for, according to John 6 : 54, "he who eats my flesh and drinks my blood has eternal life," which could not apply to Judas. After further reflection on the sixth chapter of John, which became a *locus classicus* for his entire theology, Schwenckfeld wrote *Duodecim Quaestiones oder Argumenta contra impanationem*, copies of which were sent to Luther and certain colleages in Silesia (II, 132-39; XIV, 802 ff.). His close friend, Valentine Crautwald, was deeply impressed by the arguments and incited to study the problem. After intense concentration and a phenomenon which he confessed was nothing less than a direct revelation of the Spirit itself (II, 191 ff., 304 ff.), Crautwald fathered a formula interpreting Christ's words of institution which was immediately adopted by Schwenckfeld and became normative in the theology of the Middle Way. The words "this is my body" were inverted, by a Hebraic transposition, to read: "my body is this," and the demonstrative "this" (τοῦτο, *hoc*) was interpreted in a pleonastic and spiritualized sense which gave the meaning: "my body is *this*," namely, a spiritual bread or food for the soul. "My blood of the covenant is *this*," namely, a spiritual drink for the soul (II, 205 ff., *et passim*). Since *est* was understood literally and not changed to *significat*, Schwenckfeld was ever fond of saying that in the Silesian interpretation "the *hoc* remains *hoc*, the *est est*, and the *corpus corpus*" (III, 153, 626; XII, 535).

Late in 1525 Schwenckfeld journeyed to Wittenberg in order to acquaint Luther with the Silesian view of the Eucharist.[3] Luther, however, thought the interpretation a species of Zwinglian theology and would have none of it. Accordingly, the two parted theological company, Luther relegating Schwenckfeld to the company of Carlstadt

---

[1] Cf. Loetscher, *op. cit.*, 380-85, 465-78.

[2] XIV, 802: "Ich bin wol so gut Lutherisch darbey gewest/als einer sein mag/" Cf. also I,264f.

[3] Schw.'s diary notations of this conference, II, 240-82, offer an interesting vignette of informal theological conversation in the Reformation Era.

and Zwingli as "the third head" of the sacramentarian sect,[1] and Schwenckfeld condemning any doctrine of the Lord's Supper which regarded the body of Christ as communicated "with, through, in, or by" any external element (IV, 636). In treatise after treatise he censured Luther's teaching as contrary to: Scripture, the nature of God's Word, Christian faith, the high-priesthood of Christ, the use of the early church, and, particularly, the honor and glory of God.[2] Emphasizing that the divine Lord could never be essentially present in the creaturely substance of bread, Schwenckfeld even termed the Lutheran doctrine more idolatrous than the Roman, since the essence of bread theoretically ceases to exist in transubstantiation.[3] Obviously, however, the Roman doctrine of the Eucharistic mass fared no better in Schwenckfeld's estimation (II, 58, 459; XI, 984).

As to the opposing camp in this controversy, Schwenckfeld rejected Carlstadt's interpretation out of hand (II, 358, 369; III, 60), and while at first acknowledging a certain kinship with Zwingli on the doctrine,[4] he could not accept the Swiss' *significat*. In Schwenckfeld's estimation, any variation of Christ's words in the interests of a tropic interpretation would violate their nature as spirit, life, and eternal truth itself.[5] For if the mystery and reality were removed from the words of institution

> ...a person would eat the body and blood of Christ in the Lord's Supper only *significatiue*, that is, in a figurative sense – only with the thoughts, but not in divine truth. As the prophet says, this is just as if a hungry man should dream that he ate, and, when he awakens, his soul is empty; and as if a thirsty man dreamed that he drank, and upon awakening he is weak, still thirsty, and his soul is impatient (Isa. 29 : 8; IV, 39).

In distinguishing his position from that of the Swiss, Schwenckfeld stated:

---

[1] *D. Martin Luthers Werke. Kritische Gesamtausgabe* (Weimar, 1883 ff.) (hereafter *WA*), XIX, 123.

[2] II, 475. This typical phraseology is repeated in subsequent treatises, e.g., III, 5 ff., 234 ff., 925 ff.; IX, 38 ff., *et passim*. Luther's doctrine is far and away the most frequent object of Schw.'s polemic in his many treatises on the Eucharist.

[3] X, 862; cf. also IV, 141; VII, 22.

[4] II, 442 ff.; IX, 333. See XIV, 110 ff., for Schw.'s fullest summary of his relationship to Zwingli on the doctrine of the Lord's Supper. The Swiss reformer, indeed, thought that the Silesian interpretation was comprehended in his own and, in 1528, published one of Schw.'s treatises on the Eucharist with a commendatory preface, see XIV, 106-8. Schw. rued Zwingli's action as occasioning his exile from Silesia the next year, cf. IV, 45, and Schultz, *op. cit.*, pp. 152 ff.

[5] John 6 : 63; III, 44. Cf. Schw.'s similar criticism of the views of Oecolampad, III, 77 ff. , and Berengar, III, 652.

> Briefly, however, concerning the eating of the body and the drinking of the blood of Christ there is a vast difference between us and the Zwinglians, Calvin, Bullinger, and Beza For although we say in both cases, as is certainly true, that the body and blood of Christ are eaten and drunk only spiritually, nevertheless we are indeed far from one another as to what it means that the body of Christ is *spiritually* eaten in his Supper, and his blood *spiritually* drunk.[1]

Schwenckfeld early gave definitive expression to his interpretation of the Eucharist, in which the fundamental dualism which underlies his system becomes especially evident:

> In summary, as in the sixth chapter of John, two kinds of food are to be considered in the Supper There is a twofold bread: an earthly which comes from the earth and a heavenly which comes down from heaven If the bread is twofold, there is necessarily also a twofold breaking, namely, for the external and internal man The earthly and outer bread is broken in representation for the outer man; the heavenly bread, that is, the incarnate Word of God, is broken in reality for the inner and reborn man.... This, however, takes place not merely rhetorically, as we formerly imagined: this happens through faith when I believe, etc. Nay rather truly, truly does the living Word of God, Christ the heavenly Bread, feed our soul; truly he refreshes and consoles the despairing conscience; truly does the blood of Christ.. quench eternal thirst (II, 354 f.).

The external celebration, which Schwenckfeld termed the *commemoratio*, not only memorializes Jesus' death, but serves as a symbol or demonstration that the participants experience an internal communion with Christ, a soul-nourishing consumption or *manducatio* of the very Word of God (II, 346; III, 376). Finding the precise relationship between the external and internal participation, of course, is crucial to an understanding of Schwenckfeld's view. Sometimes he insisted that the inner, spiritual communion must precede the external;[2] elsewhere he implied that the two eatings might frequently coincide (III, 721; V, 674) and should, in fact, be simultaneous in a proper observance of the sacrament (XIII, 248; XIV, 379). "I hold that in the Supper of the Lord, where it is observed according to his will, the minister outwardly distributes the bread and the cup of the Lord in commemoration of him. Christ, however, at the same time [*dabei*] innerly feeds the believers unto eternal life with his holy body and blood."[3] Again, however, the spiritual order is to be distinguished

---

[1] XIV, 116 (italics mine).

[2] II, 621: "...participatio spiritalis precedit corporalem Vel externam manducationem," for the external observance, or *Gratias*, is really a thanksgiving for the spiritual participation, IV, 637. Cf. also V, 170, where Schw. asserts that the outer *commemoratio* dare not take place unless the inner *manducatio* has preceded.

[3] XIII, 248. In view of such later references from Vols. XIII and XIV, cf. Maron, *op. cit.*,

from the material, and the two participations may or may not occur simultaneously.¹

An external celebration of the sacrament dared never take place without the internal, for, in Schwenckfeld's estimation, this would imply a failure to discern Christ's body and incur divine retribution (V, 170). But an inner communion could never occur so long as Christians regarded their Lord as essentially present in the elements (Roman Catholics, Lutherans), or did not sufficiently stress the reality of spiritual communion (the Swiss). And since the true believer could realize a spiritual celebration apart from the Lord's Table, Schwenckfeld discouraged the outer observance of the sacrament until a broad reform in doctrine and life should educate the laity, or Christ should himself re-establish the external celebration (XII, 719 f.). Schwenckfeld first advised a suspension of the Eucharist in 1526. Originally intended only as a temporary measure, his famous *Stillstand* became a permanent characteristic of the Middle Way.²

The outer communion therefore remained only a theoretical possibility with Schwenckfeld, while the inner observance received the predominating emphasis in his theology. He taught his followers that they were able to partake of Christ spiritually "every day, every hour, yes every moment." ³ If not limited in time, the inner communion was also not restricted by space. Jesus, for example, held a spiritual Supper with the Old Testament fathers (IV, 23 ff.), his disciples (John 6), Martha and the woman at the well (Luke 10; John 4; IV,

---

p. 88 "Der *frühe* Schw. kennt noch eine ausserliche commemoratio" (italics mine). Schw. held to a theoretical external celebration of the Eucharist throughout his life, even if he did not stress the *commemoratio* as much in later years.

Schw.'s earlier definitions of the Supper have an even less anti-Lutheran ring, e.g.: "...der Leyb unnd Blut Christi allen Christen ym Sacrament under der gestalt/ gleichniss/ oder eygenschafft des Brots unnd Trancks furgetragen/ von yhnen/ jm geheimnuss durch einen rechten glauben/ jm lebendigen Worte Gottes werde entphangen/ und zur speyse unnd tranck der seelen genossen/" III, 414. Cf. also III, 410, 424 ff., 630.

¹ IX, 718. "...bede beim rechten brauch des Sacraments und one denselbigen" is the most frequent formula, used *passim* by Schw.

² II, 332, 608. Cf. IV, 634, where Schw. lists his reasons for the *Stillstand*; also IV, 820; V, 687; IX, 142, 172; XII, 717; XIV, 622, and "Summarium vom Stillstand beim brauch des sacraments des Herren Nachtmals" (1561), to be published in XVI as Doc. MCLXI. The *Stillstand* was maintained from Schw.'s death until 1877, when the Schwenckfelders who emigrated to America reinstituted the outer celebration of the Lord's Supper in their worship services. Cf. Schultz, *op. cit.*, p. 111.

³ XI, 435; cf. also VI, 164; VIII, 228. In X, 413, the inner communion is described as taking place "on [ohne] unterlass."

602 f.), the blind man of John nine (VII, 357 f.), and with all who had faith in him (VII, 389).

The nature of the believer's spiritual communion was the object of Schwenckfeld's frequent, if imprecise, comment. Among other descriptive modes, he variously represented this spiritual eating and drinking as faith in Christ (III, 156), knowledge of him (X, 541), the Holy Spirit's prompting the heart of the Christian to receive, love, and obey his Lord, and the indwelling activity of Christ in the heart (XI, 702). Most frequently Schwenckfeld availed himself of the formula of Augustine, whom he cited more than any other church father on the doctrine of the Eucharist: *Qui credit in eum manducat eum.*[1] But faith, for Schwenckfeld, was a very pregnant concept, proceeding further than any orthodox definition of the term. While his doctrine will be discussed later in detail, the following passage illustrates the depth and mystical overtones involved in the Schwenckfeldian definition of spiritual communion as faith: "Eating means... partaking of the essence [*Wesen*] of Christ through true faith. The bodily food is transformed into our nature, but the spiritual food changes us into itself, that is, the divine nature, so that we become partakers of it, II, Pet. 1."[2]

Schwenckfeld also spoke of faith as ascending heavenward in spiritual communion, reminiscent of Calvin's[3] concept: "True faith soars beyond itself [*erschwingt sich*] and everything human, earthly, and visible to the right hand of God in heavenly being where Christ is... who distributes to all Christ-believing souls the heavenly treasures;

---

[1] *Opera*, ed. Basel 1505/6, IX, 6; 1.2. as quoted in III, 158, *et passim*.

[2] II, 574; cf. also IX, 226.

[3] The parallels between Schw.'s and Calvin's concepts of the Eucharist are apparent enough and have been noted. Walther Kohler, "Kaspar Schwenckfeld," *Die Religion in Geschichte und Gegenwart*, Zweite Aufl., V (1931), 355, thinks that Schw.'s doctrine of the Lord's Supper "moglicherweise durch Vermittlung von Bucer auf Calvin eingewirkt [hat]." Cf. also Loetscher, *op. cit.*, 385, 475 f., and Hampe, *op. cit.*, p. 12. It should, however, be remembered that Calvin objected to Schw.'s sundering of the signs from the spiritual realities, CR XL, 454 ff.; Schw., in turn, objected to Calvin's interpretation of *est* in the words of institution, XIV, 116, and his attaching of the signs to the reality of the sacrament, XV, 251 f. Cf. also Schw.'s critique, to be published as Doc. MLXXXVII in XVI. C. Franklin Arnold, "Zur Geschichte und Literatur der Schwenckfelder," *Zeitschrift des Vereins fur Geschichte Schlesiens*, XLIII (Breslau, 1909), 297 f., indicates a negative relationship: "Man kann es als ziemlich gewiss annehmen, dass Schwenckfeld und dessen Lehre nicht fruher als im Jahre 1545 in Calvins Gesichtskreis getreten ist.... Im folgenden Jahre polemisierte der Genfer Reformator mit Entschiedenheit gegen Schwenckfelds Abendmahlslehre.... Auch der ganze Kreis Calvins hatte fur Schwenckfeld keine Anerkennung, ja man kann sagen kein Verstandnis.... Kurz, der ursprungliche Calvinismus hat dem Schwenckfeld innerlich ferner gestanden, als das Luthertum."

where he feeds and nourishes them out of his property" (V, 205).

In discussing the practical indications and benefits of spiritual communion, Schwenckfeld stated: "As often as a man senses divine sweetness in Christ, comfort, joy, love, grace, and mercy; as often as he has a foretaste of eternal life, he holds with the Lord his Supper" (VIII, 228). The Schwenckfeldian inner Eucharist, therefore, is so broadened and subjectivized a concept that the doctrine would seem to have deteriorated into a mere tropology, expressible even in other terms, as in the above citation. And yet spiritual communion *as faith*, whose mystical implications will be discussed subsequently, pertains to the very core of Schwenckfeld's system.

Baptism

The reformer's doctrine of baptism [1] follows a pattern parallel to his understanding of the Lord's Supper. Although he gave some concern to the problem of infant baptism in his earlier career, Schwenckfeld generally devoted much less thought to this sacrament. For a time he did not question pedobaptism or baptism as a means of grace even after he had broken with Wittenberg on the doctrine of the Lord's Supper.[2] Once again, however, it was popular ignorance in regard to the sacrament and particularly the question of infant baptism which called forth Schwenckfeld's investigation and protest. In 1527 he and Crautwald jointly complained to the Bishop of Breslau that too often the officiant, child, sponsors, and parents knew as much about the true significance of baptism as did the water, salt, and baptismal font (II, 657). Three years later Schwenckfeld wrote a treatise incorporating sixteen arguments against the pedobaptism which he had formerly "loved, praised, and defended."[3] Indeed he soon asserted:

> .. I regard the baptism of infants to be the beginning of papistry and the foundation of all error and ignorance in the church of Christ, and, moreover, the destruction of all piety and... the apostolic ministry. I am not able

---

[1] Cf. Hans Urner, "Die Taufe bei Caspar Schwenckfeld," *Theologische Literaturzeitung*, VI (1948), 329-42; Erich Seeberg, "Der Gegensatz zwischen Zwingli, Schwenckfeld, und Luther," *Reinhold-Seeberg-Festschrift* (Leipzig, 1929), I, 57-63, on the relationship of the Spirit to baptism; and Karl Ecke, *Das Ratsel der Taufe* (Gutersloh, 1952), pp. 21 ff.

[2] II, 97, 331. The first Silesian attack on the efficacy of external baptism as a means of grace in the Lutheran sense seems to have come from the pen of Crautwald, II, 403 ff., "Brevis Monitio Eorvm, Qvi in Evcharistia Dei Verbvm in Pane, et in Baptismate verbum esse in acqua, asserunt" (1526?).

[3] III, 813 ff.; quotation from IV, 243.

to think otherwise, with a good conscience, until I shall have been better informed from the Scriptures (III, 858).

Schwenckfeld later maintained that for a thousand years the Christian church had not administered the sacrament of baptism correctly (VII, 252).

According to the presuppositions of Schwenckfeld's system, on the one hand a concern regarding infant baptism appears warranted because of his insistence that the external sacrament dared not take place without the internal (VII, 429). On the other hand, since grace could not be conveyed through any outer means, we might anticipate that Schwenckfeld would not concern himself excessively with the physical baptismal rite in general, not to say pedobaptism. A vacillation did, in fact, occur in his theological development. Although Schwenckfeld had been firm in his insistence that pedobaptism was totally unscriptural and unwarranted, subsequently he refused anabaptism as a corrective (IV, 795), stated that infant baptism did not concern him (IV, 794; V, 387), and finally agreed that pedobaptism – including his own – sufficed so far as the external rite was concerned (VII, 69), although he never encouraged its administration.[1]

By substituting "water" for "bread and wine," and "washing" for "eating and drinking" in the previous citations on Schwenckfeld's interpretation of the Eucharist, we will arrive at his doctrine of baptism as well. Once again there are two waters and two washings: the external and the internal. The physical washing must not be regarded as mere outward ceremonial, the failing of the Anabaptists (IV, 121 ff.), but, on the other hand, the mystery and promise in the sacrament must not be conjoined to the water, the fault of the "scribes" (i.e., Lutherans, VII, 430). Each washing can function only within its own order:

> In summary, the inner baptism of the Holy Spirit comforts, strengthens, and assures the believing soul or inner man. The outer baptism of the man or minister, however, comforts, strengthens, and assures the believing flesh or outer man, so that the whole man is comforted, assured, and blessed. The external assurance, however, requires the priority of the internal (VII, 450).

> Concerning baptism, I hold that the minister in the course of grace baptizes with water, but Jesus Christ baptizes with the Holy Spirit (XIII, 248).

Again, Schwenckfeld considers it ideal when the two washings coincide:

> If now these two [the Word and water] come together sacramentally in a

---

[1] For Schw.'s views on the fate of the infant dead, cf. VIII, 93; IX, 428; XIV, 393.

> divine transaction so that each proceeds correctly in its order and is understood and received in faith according to the institution of Christ, then the whole sacrament and mystery is accomplished and well applied, wherein also the whole new man – for whom alone the sacraments are instituted – is cleansed both internally and externally, and washed from the pollution of the soul and body (VII, 440 f.).

Once again it is the *inner* washing which has the true significance in Schwenckfeld's theology, and he concerns himself predominantly with spiritual baptism. The concept of an internal ablution, however, is not alluded to nearly so frequently as that of spiritual communion in the Lord's Supper. It is, in fact, virtually replaced by a parallel emphasis on spiritual regeneration, rebirth, and the origin of the new man through the indwelling of Christ.

CHAPTER V

DOCTRINE OF THE WORD

The doctrine of the Word of God in Schwenckfeld's theology [1] is consistent with his concept of the sacraments. According to the familiar pattern, there is an inner and outer Word, gospel, preacher, ears, and hearing, corresponding to the inner and outer man.[2] The true, eternal, natural Word of God is spirit and life (John 6), and none other than Christ himself. The transitory, external letter is "word of God" only in a derived sense, whether written in Scripture, spoken in the sermon, or portrayed in symbol, picture, and sign.[3] Once again, the internal and the external word must be distinguished in separate orders: the inner Word is not conveyed by means of the outer and can brook no mixture with the external.[4] But here again there can be a simultaneous communication, the outer word declaring, announcing, and pointing to the inner Word, Christ (II, 485; III, 174; IV, 132 f.). The function of the outer word, however, pertains primarily to the external order, for it is a "...promise and sign given to believers only for the instruction and assurance of their flesh and external man, and as a reminder and demonstration of inner faith, even as it must be understood only from and through faith" (II, 687).

Christ as inner Word, on the other hand, is represented by Schwenckfeld according to his various spiritual functions as: the *seed* which

[1] For this *locus*, see especially Grutzmacher, *Wort und Geist*, pp. 158-73; also J. H. Maronier, *Het Inwendig Woord* (Amsterdam, 1890), pp. 51-79. The latter gives an accurate portrayal, but does not sufficiently discuss the differences between Schw.'s concept of the inner Word and that of Hans Denk and Sebastian Franck. Schw. and Franck are better contrasted in J. Lindeboom, *Stiefkinderen van het Christendom* ('s-Gravenhage, 1929), pp. 164-90, esp. 182 f.; and Reinhold Pietz, *Der Mensch Ohne Christus, Eine Untersuchung zur Anthropologie Caspar Schwenckfelds* (Unpublished dissertation, University of Tubingen, 1956), pp. 106-22, who has made the most detailed study of the problem. Cf. also Alfred Hegler, *Geist und Schrift bei Sebastian Franck* (Freiburg i.B., 1892), pp. 276-80.

[2] II, 485; III, 354; IX, 457; XII, 510; XIII, 308, *et passim*.

[3] Schw. had made this distinction already in 1524, II, 40 ff.; cf. also II, 455, *et passim*. Of greatest influence on his division of the inner and outer Word were Augustine – cf., e.g., XI, 385, and J. P. Migne, *Patrologiae, Series latina* (here after *MSL*) 35, col. 1609 ff. – and Tauler, cf. XIV, 349 ff., *et infra*.

[4] II, 454, 485; II, 569. "Cursus verbi dei vivi, liber est, non haeret in visibilibus... sed totus in invisibilibus quiescit," from Schw.'s basic treatise, *De Cursu Verbi Dei* (1527).

regenerates the new, inner man (IX, 461); the *bread* or *food* which nourishes the reborn soul as it grows (IX, 461 ff.); the *water* which washes away the sins of the regenerate and quenches the thirst of his soul (IX, 463 ff.); *spirit*, not letter (IX, 466 f.); *life* and *light* (IX, 467 f.); and the *word of the cross* (IX, 469 f.). Clearly, then, the activity of Christ in the spiritual sphere of both sacrament and Word is essentially identical: in his immediacy with the believing soul or inner man, Christ is his own means of grace; and the grace which he communicates is himself.

The Bible

As to the written word, the Holy Scriptures in Schwenckfeldian theology are regarded as inspired by the Holy Spirit,[1] inerrant (IV, 107), and normative for Christian faith and life (III, 679; XII, 426, 451). Inspiration, however, is not understood as any mechanistic process. The Bible is merely the recorded likeness or adumbration of that which was worked in the hearts of the prophets and apostles by revelation of the Spirit (XIII, 222 f.). Yet Schwenckfeld always advocated the ardent reading of Holy Scripture, and the lengthy indices of Biblical citations at the end of each volume in the *Corpus Schwenckfeldianorum* amply demonstrate his own constant recourse to the Scriptures.

The decisive consideration, of course, is the hermeneutical. Despite occasional unfortunate allegorization, Schwenckfeld generally held to a christocentric exegetical norm, viz.: "The exposition of all texts in Holy Scripture should and must be sought and understood in the one Christ, in whom all the treasures of wisdom are hidden."[2] Hence the demonstrative function of the Bible: "The Scriptures... indicate, indeed, who and what the Word of God is, but do not pass themselves off for that Word. They always point beyond themselves to Christ, who must preach and utter himself into the believing heart through the Holy Spirit, and who alone is the Word, Power, and Wisdom of God" (V, 126).

The entire Bible, therefore, is oriented to Christ, and its true exposition requires "scholars of God" rather than "of the letter."[3] To

---

[1] "eingesprochen," XIV, 1005; cf. also III, 726 ff.

[2] III, 44. Cf. also V, 497: "Man muss auch auff dieses einige stuck der Menschwerdung des ewigen Sons Gottes/ unnd der Gottwerdung des Sons des Menschen inn Gott/ die gantze heilige Schrifft richten/" For Schw.'s best summary of his hermeneutics, see VII, 642-47.

[3] IV, 62-65; VIII, 91 ff. (The contrast between "Gottesgelehrten" and "Schriftgelehrten" is a favorite with Schw.) The subjectivity implicit in such a view of Scripture occasionally comes to the fore in the *Corpus*. In one of his last writings, "Rechenschafft Von Caspar Schwenck-

summarize, Schwenckfeld's views bespeak a mediating spiritualism: the Holy Scriptures constitute the norm of theology, but only a spiritual understanding of the Bible is its normative interpretation. The inner Word is the ultimate Expositor, but his exposition necessarily corresponds to the outer word, even if the two are not instrumentally correlated.[1]

The Ministry

Schwenckfeld's doctrine of the ministry is rooted in his assumption that the spoken word is no more a *vehiculum* of the inner Word than is the written word. While the apostolic ministry did possess divine efficacy, the apostles themselves were unable to communicate their spiritual power (X, 613), and the office had degenerated considerably since their day.[2] Yet Schwenckfeld never advised the suspension of the ministry, as he did the outer celebration of the Lord's Supper, but respected the office if administered according to the will of God.[3] Indeed, even if preaching itself never involved a means of grace in the Lutheran sense, it was necessary positively because the outer man needed such instruction – the inner could receive the Holy Spirit "without, with, and during the sermon" (XII, 50) – and negatively since it served as a curb against popular tumult (XIII, 359). Schwenckfeld grouped ministers into three classes: 1) true servants of the word of God – the prophets, evangelists, apostles, and all those taught and sent by God, in whose ministry the Trinity itself is active; 2) servants of the Holy Scriptures – those who direct their hearers to Christ and interpret the Bible christocentrically, but whose function cannot be

---

felds Vocation/ Beruff Lauff und Lere" (1561), to be published in XVI as Doc. MCLXVI, Schw. could make the statement "Wir konnen zum lob und preiss der gnaden Gottes nicht bergen/ Das unser leere/ nicht allein auss der h. schrifft/ sonder mehr auss der gnedigen offenbarung Gottes des Vatters und lebendigen worts ist."

[1] XII, 451. "Es muss alles der Hailigen schrifft gemess sein und damit stimmen/ was der gaist innerlich im hertzen leret."

[2] Cf., e g., II, 7J "Es sein schier alle bierheuser vol unnutzer prediger/ lassen sich beduncken so sie nur ainen zanck mit gotes wort anrichten widerpart halten kunden und ser schreyhen sauffen und alle eyttelkait treiben/ es stund gantz wol in der Christenhait man redte stetigs von gotte/ sagen sie steen bey gottes worte;" also V, 141 f , where Schw. lists twenty deficiencies of the preachers.

[3] In X, 720, Schw. calls the ministry "ain herrlich hoch selig ampt." Some have enlarged on Schw.'s de-emphasis of externals into a sweeping rejection of them, e.g , Otto Borngraber, *Das Erwachen der philosophischen Spekulation der Reformationszeit* (Erlangen, 1908), p. 23 "Die Verwerfung aller ausseren Gnadenmittel, ja, alles objectiven Kirchentums, auch des offentlichen Predigamts ist nur die negative Konsequenz dieser [Schw.'s] Subjektivitats- oder Erfahrungsreligion."

compared with the high apostolic office; 3) servants of the letter – the *Schriftgelehrten*, who suspend the work of the Holy Spirit and show few fruits for their labors (XII, 442 ff.).

The Church

Finally, Schwenckfeld's concept of the church [1] is analogous to his doctrine of Word and sacrament. Again there is an internal and external church: the former, the true, universal body of Christ, the full number of the elect (IV, 183; VIII, 463); the latter, the outer establishments which include both genuine believers and hypocrites. Members of the true body of Christ may or may not be listed on congregational rolls, and their salvation does not depend upon membership in the visible churches nor on partaking of the means which they dispense.[2] Early in his career Schwenckfeld stated that there was no true Christian church in Germany (II, 171), or at least none which could correspond to the apostolic pattern laid down by Paul and Peter (II, 218; IV, 817). While condemning no particular body, Schwenckfeld was concerned about where to find the Christian church when "the Papists damn the Lutherans; the Lutherans damn the Zwinglians... the Zwinglians damn the Anabaptists, and the Anabaptists damn all the others" (IV, 818). One of the most important reasons Schwenckfeld gave for the observance of a sacramental *Stillstand* was his conviction that only a true external church could have the privilege of dispensing the sacraments (IV, 185). Since he did not find such a genuine congregation anywhere, he set his hopes on a future church which, established by the Spirit, would be characterized by the unity, purity, and charismatic gifts of the early Christian church (II, 280; IX, 905). But until such a church were established, he did not, as a rule, advise his followers against attending the Lutheran services (XII, 796). For the present they were to constitute pious *ecclesiolae in ecclesia*.

Although this aspect of Schwenckfeld's theology has been in-

---

[1] For Schw.'s ecclesiology, cf. Ecke, *Schwenckfeld, Luther, etc.*, pp. 99-227. According to Ecke's thesis, Schw. is "der Wiederentdecker der charismatischen Organisation des apostolischen Zeitalters...," p. 109, and the voice crying for ecumenicity in the wilderness of schism in the Reformation Era, p. 214 ff. For a penetrating approach, emphasizing the individualistic and separatistic principle in Schw.'s concept of the church, see Maron, *op. cit.*, pp. 114-49; 177-83. Maron posits, and correctly, subjective *Innerlichkeit* as the quintessence of Schw.'s thought world, but sometimes draws conclusions which would likely have startled Schw. himself, e.g., p. 186.

[2] III, 902 ff. Cf. also VIII, 474, and XI, 97, where Schw. characterizes true Christians as in a state of dispersion.

vestigated more thoroughly than any of his other doctrines, the concept of the church does not bulk large in the writings or system of the lay theologian. His ecclesiology is not well developed, and his attitude toward the external churches vacillating. Schwenckfeld had neither the capacity nor the occasion for organizing his followers; but any deficiency in this respect may be balanced by the fact that he did not wish to father a fifth church in Christendom.[1]

[1] IV, 831; V, 28 ff.; XIII, 161-63; XIV, 15. At the time of Schw.'s death, his followers numbered some 4000. The last person in Europe who confessed himself a Schwenckfelder died in Lower Silesia in 1826. Driven out of this area in 1720 by a Jesuit mission, most of the Schwenckfelders moved to Pennsylvania in America, where they still exist today as a separate church body numbering above 2000. For a history of the Schwenckfelders, see Kadelbach, *op. cit.*, pp. 16 ff.; Ecke, *op. cit.*, pp. 227-85; 295-323; and H. W. Kriebel, *The Schwenckfelders in Pennsylvania* (Lancaster, Pa., 1904).

PART II
THE CHRISTOLOGICAL FOCUS

CHAPTER VI

DERIVATION OF SCHWENCKFELD'S
DOCTRINE OF THE PERSON AND WORK OF CHRIST

To explore adequately those origins of Schwenckfeld's Christology and soteriology which lie beyond the presuppositions and demands of his own system would require a separate study. Nevertheless, a brief overview of the reformer's theological background is indicated. Fundamentally characteristic of his thought world was a Pauline, and even more strongly, a Johannine Biblicism. Indeed, Schwenckfeld's spiritual interpretation of the Scriptures remained the ultimate norm for his theology.

Of the Greek fathers he read especially Cyril, Naziansus, Athanasius, Origen, Epiphanius, and Irenaeus; of the Latin, Augustine, Ambrose, Hilary, Tertullian, Rufinus, Cassian, and Jerome. The precise nature of patristic influences on Schwenckfeld's christological doctrines will be indicated separately as the several theologoumena arise in the following discussion. Here we may summarize by saying that Alexandrian theology, as represented by Cyril, greatly influenced Schwenckfeld in its stress on the unity and glory of the person of Christ, his immediacy, and the believer's participation in him. In the west, Augustine, but especially Hilary and Ambrose with their emphasis on the person and work of Christ in the state of exaltation were most frequently cited by Schwenckfeld in support of his Christology and soteriology.

As for the medieval theologians, Schwenckfeld consulted particularly the works of the German mystics. While the *Theologia Germanica* remained of only tertiary significance for him, the *Imitatio Christi* had considerable effect on his ethics. Probably the greatest influence on his theology, however, was that exerted by Johannes Tauler. To him much of the dualism in Schwenckfeld's system is likely attributable (XII, 141 ff.); his Christology and soteriology also bear significant traces of Tauler's influence, as we shall note.[1]

Among Schwenckfeld's contemporaries Luther was the dominant

[1] For a more detailed discussion of Schw.'s historical connection with the mystics, see chap. XI, *infra*.

influence in his theological development until he broke with the reformer and read Tauler and Cyril instead. Staupitz, Carlstadt, and Münzer may have had some small effect in reinforcing the spiritualistic aspects of Schwenckfeld's theology, but they had no influence on his Christology. Finally, his close friend and associate, Valentine Crautwald, who proved as original as Schwenckfeld in developing certain phases of Silesian theology – particularly the doctrine of the Lord's Supper – was more the systematic commentator than the creative genius in the Christology and soteriology of the Middle Way (V, 747, 757, 765 ff.; VII, 126).

Schwenckfeld's interest in Christology developed directly and inevitably from his prior concentration on the doctrine of the Eucharist. It became his early, existential concern that both he and the common Christian know precisely where to find the Lord, "whether in bread, or in cup, or in heaven" (II, 371 f.). Schwenckfeld and Crautwald reasoned that the dwelling place of the Word, which is spirit, must also be spiritual and therefore beyond the creatural, materiality and finitude of bread, wine, or water (II, 404). Repeatedly they asserted against the Lutheran doctrine of the Eucharist that to confess the body of Christ as present in bread was to regard the creature as God (II-V, *et passim*). In Schwenckfeld's thought world, this would have involved an intolerable breach between the realms of the spiritual-divine and the physical-creaturely. He carried this dualism directly into his Christology, and this, ultimately, is the key which explains many of his singular opinions concerning the person and work of Christ. Christology, however, with its fundamental doctrine of the incarnation of God in creaturely man appeared to violate the very cosmological dualism which Schwenckfeld had so faithfully maintained in opposition to a *Gnadenmittel* theology. At first he did, indeed, admit that in Christ the Creator had, once and only once, suspended the dualism which he had established and united with the creature: "Besides the union of the Word of God with the flesh there can be no other essential union of God and the creature." [1] But Schwenckfeld innerly recoiled at the thought that the divine could have become conjoined with the creaturely, despite the stubborn fact of the Incarnation.

---

[1] II, 481. The statement of the ed. of the *CS* in VI, 86 needs revision. "Schwenckfeld maintained that Christ's humanity was deified, Jesus was not a creature.... This position was maintained by Schwenckfeld from the beginning to the end of his career." Besides the passage from II, 481, Christ is also unqualifiedly designated a creature, with the implication that the creaturely status pertains also to the state of exaltation, in II, 520; cf. also III, 360. References after this qualify Christ's creaturity to the state of humiliation, *vide infra*.

His scruples in this regard were, indeed, consistent with his dualistic opposition to a means of grace. For logically there was no qualitative difference between the Creator's use of created flesh in the case of the Incarnation and his possible utilization of creaturely externals in a means of grace according to the Lutheran sense. That God should have united with the creature, man, was no less a dishonor to his majesty than if he should combine with created bread in the Lord's Supper. But the burden of Schwenckfeld's opposition to the Lutheran *Gnadenmittel* had been to save God's honor by wresting the divine presence and grace from any attachment to creaturely externals. The infinite majesty of the Creator precluded any such combination with the limitation and materiality of his creation.

Obviously Schwenckfeld had no high opinion of the term "creature." He agreed with his opponents that the word was defined, "that which God created out of nothing and whatever proceeds from it." [1] But the connotations and attributes which Schwenckfeld predicated of creaturity [2] had one common denominator: antithesis to the divine. Not only was the creature subject to such non-divine characteristics as finitude, materiality, locality, alterability, sickness, death, and decay, but, apart from God's intervention, was also ontologically separated from the Creator by the familiar cosmic dualism in Schwenckfeld's system. A final reason why the reformer balked at attributing creaturity to the humanity of Jesus stemmed from the fact that he sundered holiness – this must be understood as *non posse peccare* – from anything creaturely: "No creature is formed holy according to its nature, as we also know that true holiness has its origin not in the work of creation, but in grace and from the birth, nature, and essence of God." [3]

Schwenckfeld therefore concluded that the divine and the creaturely were mutually exclusive, as separate as the spiritual and the material, as removed as heaven and earth. "In short, God and creature cannot endure or tolerate each other in one person." [4] Accordingly, we shall note how the term "creature" as an attribute of Christ's humanity became progressively distasteful to Schwenckfeld.

By the end of 1528 he stated that the designation could not

---

[1] VII, 507. For a more extensive definition, cf. VII, 533, 562.

[2] This word is coined in preference to dictionary listings of "creaturehood", "creatureliness," or "creatureship."

[3] VII, 547. Schw.'s virtual identification of creaturity and sin will be discussed *infra* in connection with his anthropology.

[4] VII, 506. "Mit kurtzem/ Gott und Creatur mogen sich in einer person keins wegs vertragen/ noch einander dulden." Cf. also VII, 548, *et passim*.

properly be predicated of Jesus in the state of exaltation, but only in the sate of humiliation.[1] In 1537 Schwenckfeld was no longer satisfied to refer to Jesus even in the state of humiliation as a mere creature, without further qualification:

> It is true that while he was here on earth, Christ Jesus belonged to the creaturely order, nature, and name even as other men, although without sin.... But he was a *new creature*, a new man, conceived by the Holy Spirit and born of the Virgin Mary; a new man, through whom and from whom the new birth and all other new men have their origin.[2]

But how, logically, could even a new creature become a non-creature? Inevitably, Schwenckfeld's opposition to the term reached its obvious conclusion when, in August, 1538,[3] he finally claimed that even in the state of humiliation Christ could not correctly be termed a creature:

> Although the man, Jesus, by reason of the physical birth of his flesh, was also included here on earth in the order of the essence of earthly man... yet he does not belong in this old creaturely order of creation, but in the new order of recreation or rebirth (VI, 136).

Even the expressions "new creature" or "heavenly creature" were rejected as inadequate ascriptions for the earthly Christ.[4]

The denial of the creaturity of Jesus' humanity both in the states of exaltation and humiliation became one of the *nova* in Schwenckfeld's system and constituted his point of separation from orthodox Christology. Repeatedly he maintained, however, that his concern with the doctrine of Christ was dictated by something more than a logomachy over the word creature. It was the nature, substance, and qualities connoted in the term which concerned Schwenckfeld and plunged him into a christological controversy which terminated only with his death.

The other major incentive from the Eucharistic dispute which proved so determinative in the development of Schwenckfeld's Christology and soteriology was the question as to how the risen and

---

[1] III, 390. Schw. also restricted creaturity to Jesus' state of humiliation in the following refs.: II, 409, 558, 700; IV, 18, 647; V, 340, 464, 784.

[2] V, 793, italics mine.

[3] Not 1539, as Maronier, *op. cit.*, p. 55: "In 1539 verkondigde hij voor het eerst deze leer...."

[4] Later Schw. conceded occasionally that Jesus might be called a "new creature" in the state of humiliation because of his mortality, but that any such characterization should never be applied to the glorified Lord. He himself would not call the earthly Jesus a "new creature." Cf. VI, 571· "Wiewol man jhnen nu an solchem orte etwas darbey mocht nachlassen/ wenn sie sagten: Dass Christus daselbs/ da Er noch sterblich war/ ein Creatur gewest sey/ so ferr sie es erclarten/ und darbey sagten ein newe/ Creatur/ und nit schlecht anhin ein Creatur/" Cf. also VII, 285 f., 864; IX, 111; XI, 743; XII, 614.

glorified Lord could commune the believer with his true body and blood. That the Word or divine nature of Christ could so nourish the heart and soul of the Christian posed no difficulty, since it was spiritual by nature. But, with Luther, Schwenckfeld maintained that the humanity of Jesus was eminently involved in the process if believers were actually to partake of his flesh and blood in something more than a tropological sense. What, then, was the nature of the flesh communicated in the Eucharist, and what was the mode of its communication? Schwenckfeld rejected Luther's recourse to the ubiquity of Christ's body as absurd and pantheistic (X, 702); nevertheless, he proposed a related solution.

Beginning *ca.* 1528, Schwenckfeld developed his famous doctrine of the deification (*Vergottung*) of Christ's humanity.[1] Its connection with the Lord's Supper is clear. The earthly body of Jesus, circumscribed as it was within the material order, finite, and physically accessible only to the senses, had to undergo a deification, an essential transformation into the spiritual order, so that, in unity with the Word, it could nourish the spiritual part of the believer, i.e., his heart and soul. Although, however, Schwenckfeld might oppose the creaturity of Christ on principle and by theoretical argument,[2] he could not similarly dispose of Jesus' material flesh during his earthly ministry without being guilty of the grossest Docetism. Nor did he ever make such an attempt. Rather, Schwenckfeld sharply emphasized the essential difference between Christ's states of humiliation and exaltation. The former he regarded as of comparatively less value to the believer because the flesh of Jesus was circumscribed by terrestrial limitations. But with the resurrection, ascension, and session, presaged to a degree even during Christ's lifetime, the humanity of Jesus was glorified, deified, and changed into a heavenly nature, which, although in full equality and unity with the divine nature, nevertheless retains its genuine humanity. Through this spiritual body the Lord is enabled to nourish the believer in any age with his true flesh and blood. The deification of Christ's humanity is the core doctrine of Schwenckfeld's Christology-soteriology, and, in turn, of his entire theology. Along with the concept of the non-creaturity of

---

[1] References to the necessity of knowing the divine glory of Christ's exalted flesh appear even before this, however; cf. II, 450, 523, 527, 553, 573 (1527). Hirsch, *op. cit.*, p. 165, places Schw.'s first more definite pronouncements on this theologoumenon a little too late, i.e. IV, 763 f. (1533). Earlier refs. include III, 212 (1528); III, 887 f. (1530); and IV, 20, 30 (1530).

[2] *Vide infra.*

Jesus, it constitutes a *novum* in Schwenckfeld's contribution to the Christology of the Reformation Era.

Once the Eucharistic controversy had directed his attention to the doctrine of Christ, however, Schwenckfeld's theologizing in this *locus* was by no means limited merely to explaining the nature and mode in which the body of Jesus was communicated in the sacrament. Rather, his preoccupation shifted from the doctrine of the Eucharist to the Christology in which it was comprehended. And here Schwenckfeld's primary concern became the believer's genuine, experiential understanding and apprehension of the present, exalted Lord.

In this regard, theological concerns parallel to the doctrine of the Lord's Supper also guided the christological development of Schwenckfeld. The popular ethical deficiencies which he deplored indicated that the relationship between Christ and the individual Christian needed clarification and improvement. The whole tone of Schwenckfeld's doctrine of Word and sacrament emphasized the spiritual nature of this affinity and an immediacy which could ultimately dispense with externals. But before such a relationship could become an established reality, the believer had to be able to recognize, know, and apprehend the immediate Christ. Schwenckfeld therefore understood as his task the identification and description of what became the lodestar of his theology: the person and work of the present, reigning, glorified Lord.

To his contemporaries, most of whom made but a feeble effort to understand Schwenckfeldian Christology, serious theological inquiry into the person of the glorified Christ seemed little more than unwarranted curiosity and sophistry. Schwenckfeld, however, protested that he was driven by genuinely practical, and not idle speculative, considerations. Knowledge of the radiant and reigning Lord was the salvation not only of the scholar but of the layman as well. Believers had to recognize the glorious Object of their faith, prayer, and worship if these activities were not to become false and meaningless. The Christian was also to nourish the high hope of being exalted with his Lord. For if, in fact, the believer would recapitulate in his own person a process of glorification analogous to that of Christ, then the knowledge of his Lord's deified humanity became a crucial and existential matter indeed.[1]

Finally, Schwenckfeld deemed the *Erkenntnis Christi* a soteriological

---

[1] Cf. "Eemanunge zum waren un seligmachende Erkanthnus Christi" (1539), VI, 508 ff., in which Schw. lists twenty arguments in defense of his christological investigations. Cf. also VII, 523.

necessity for the Christian also because the Lord's glorified humanity constituted the nexus between his person and work and the believer. Only a spiritualized flesh of Jesus could reside in the human heart and justify it by that indwelling.[1] The problem of the individual's subjective appropriation of Christ, therefore, became the guiding soteriological concern which shaped and, in turn, was shaped by Schwenckfeld's Christology.

The historical events immediately surrounding the development of Schwenckfeld's doctrine of Christ may briefly be summarized. As has been noted, occasional passages appear in his treatises prior to 1535 which deny the creaturity of Christ in the state of exaltation.[2] On May 28, 1535, a colloquy took place in the castle at Tubingen between Martin Butzer, Martin Frecht (Lutheran preacher at Ulm), Ambrosius Blaurer (Reformed pastor in Constance), and Schwenckfeld. Although the aim and the results of this conference were largely irenic and signalled a temporary truce between Schwenckfeld and the evangelical clergy of south Germany, during the course of the debate Frecht challenged Schwenckfeld's denial of Christ's creaturity in the state of exaltation and accused him of according Jesus too much honor (V, 340). This provoked most of the discussion at the colloquy, and from this date the letters and treatises of Schwenckfeld concerned themselves with Christology to an ever greater degree. An epistolatory controversy between Frecht and Schwenckfeld was followed by an open debate between the two before the council of Ulm on January 13, 1539 (VI, 398-427). Frecht then attended the convention at Schmalkalden in March, 1540, and, according to Schwenckfeld, largely secured the adoption of the articles condemning his christological doctrines (VII, 457 f.).

Meanwhile Joachim von Watt, or Vadian, the burgomaster-reformer of St. Gallen in Switzerland, now also entered the lists against Schwenckfeld. In

---

[1] XII, 654, *et infra*. Baur, "Mystik, etc.," p. 527, is hardly justified in criticizing Erbkam and Hahn for drawing Schw.'s Christology out of the Eucharistic controversy rather than from his mystical concept of justification. So also Loetscher, *op. cit.*, p. 357. "...there can be no doubt that in the main his [Baur's] strictures upon Hahn and Erbkam are borne out by the facts." In the following refs. Schw. implies or states explicitly that his Christology developed directly from the Eucharistic controversy III, 629; V, 263; VI, 132, 496, 572; VII, 525, 575, 581; VIII, 600, *et passim*. To be sure, the doctrine of justification does have some bearing on Schw.'s early christological development, but the major impulse, we must insist, derived from the Eucharistic controversy. The first extended expression of Schw.'s doctrine of essential- rather than imputative-justification came in 1530 with his discussion of Art. IV of the *Confessio Augustana* (III, 890-92). By this time, however, most of the incentive to a further study of Christology had already been provided him by the Eucharistic controversy. Moreover, Schw. did not again deal systematically with justification until 1543, from which time the doctrine bulks progressively larger in his treatises until his death. While there are, indeed, early indications that Schw.'s understanding of justification by faith differed decidedly from the Lutheran concept, cf. II, 227, 504, 506, the more mystical aspects of his doctrine of essential, rather than Luther's forensic, justification were actually developed some time *after* the break with Wittenberg had been effected.

[2] *supra*, pp. 35 ff.

July, 1539, Bullinger published his *Orthodoxa Epistola* which opposed Schwenckfeld's position, maintaining that Christ was a creature in glory so far as his humanity was concerned (VII, 454 f). The next year Vadian wrote *Antilogia, ad clarissimi viri Dom. Gasparis Schuenckfeldij argumenta* on the same theme, and *Anacephaleosis* in 1541. Responding to this challenge, Schwenckfeld prepared what, next to his great *Confession*, was his most important and systematic theological treatise, *Vom Fleische Christi* (1540).[1] Late in the following year, he completed his public apology and refutation against Vadian and Schmalkalden, the voluminous *Confession unnd Erclerung vom Erkandnus Christi und seiner Gottlichen Herrlicheit*. Schwenckfeld sent copies of this lengthy book[2] to Philip of Hesse, the city councils of Ulm, Nürnberg, and Strassburg, Vadian, the clergy of Zurich, and, indirectly, to Luther and Melanchthon.

Until 1553 Schwenckfeld's writings were dominated by christological themes in support of the *Confession*. His chief opponents continued to be the Swiss rather than the Lutherans, although he did have an extended dispute with the Lutheran Sebastian Coccius of Hall in Swabia, who wrote four books against Schwenckfeld's Christology. After 1546 and until his death, the reformer also devoted much thought to anthropology and soteriology as necessary complements to his Christology. Another major concern in this later period of Schwenckfeld's life was his famed controversy with Matthias Flacius Illyricus on the doctrine of the Word of God.[3]

[1] VII, 281-361. Unpublished until twenty-three years after his death, this treatise was circulated among Schw.'s friends and followers in MS. form.

[2] Four hundred printed pages in the *CS*, VII, 484-884.

[3] Cf. XIII-XV; also Wilhelm Preger, *Matthias Flacius Illyricus und seine Zeit* (Erlangen, 1859), pp. 298-353.

CHAPTER VII

ANTHROPOLOGICAL PRESUPPOSITIONS

Schwenckfeld summarized all of theology and salvation itself as consisting in a twofold *Erkenntnis*: 1) a knowledge of self; and 2) the knowledge of Christ.[1] True understanding of self, recognition of the fact that man is lost without a Savior, Schwenckfeld regarded as the first necessary step toward salvation. His Christology and soteriology, therefore, rested upon definite anthropological presuppositions which we must first understand in order to comprehend his doctrine of the person and work of Christ.[2]

According to the Schwenckfeldian system, God from eternity selected man alone out of all creation to share in his image, essence, nature, life, spirit, and glory (VII, 288). "In the beginning... God created humanity in order that he might dwell, walk, and live therein, and establish his essential image and kingdom in the flesh." [3]

Even before the fall, however, Adam was not the true, ideal, or perfect man which God had intended for this participation (XII, 87). He was sinless, to be sure, but he had the capacity to sin (*posse peccare*). Yet more significant was the fact of Adam's creaturity, which for Schwenckfeld connoted separation from God, antithesis to the divine, and even a negation of the concept of true humanity, i.e., man as participant in the divine nature (IV, 646; XV, 170). Was not Adam even before the fall, then, doomed to a dualistic separation from God by the very fact of his creaturity? No, because God from creation had willed to suspend man's terrestrial creaturity through Christ:

> The good and almighty God created the first man on earth earthly through his co-omnipotent Word. He did not create him so that he should remain in this state permanently, but that he might become heavenly through Christ.... When then God the Lord, after the creation of man, began to

---

[1] IX, 564; cf. also VI, 525; IX, 672; XIV, 252.
[2] Cf. Pietz, *op. cit.*, who has done a creditable task in isolating Schw.'s doctrine of natural man, particularly in the areas of the *Urstand*, free will, the conscience, and hamartiology.
[3] IV, 686; cf. also IV, 645-47; VI, 405.

conform him internally to his image ¹ and wished further to develop Adam, the earthly man, along came Doctor Satan and destroyed the work of God through his false teaching ²

The fall ruined the entire nature of man – his body, soul, heart, and conscience – and occasioned the original sin which immediately inhered within the very substance of natural and creaturely humanity.³ The presence now of essential sin in man, in addition to creaturity, precluded any God-given propensity of his to participate in the divine nature. And failing in such participation signified that man had not realized true humanity before God. He became instead totally depraved flesh, outwardly committing the sins and transgressions which were motivated internally by original sin – this Schwenckfeld identified as the inherited, inner sin of the heart, will, and desires (VIII, 192 ff.; IX, 547). Fallen man was a slave of the Devil (II, 479 ff.; X, 692 ff.) and subject to the wrath of God. Indeed, Schwenckfeld exceeded even Luther in stressing the enormity of original sin and the total depravity of man.⁴

Fallen humanity, therefore, was doubly separated from God: *cosmologically*, by the fact of man's utter creaturity over against his Creator; and *ethically*, by the presence of essential sin in man.⁵ But if

¹ From this and the previous citation in the text, it will be noted that Schw. understood the *imago Dei* not as the concomitant of man's creation, but the *remedium* of that creation: participation in the divine nature. Cf. Pietz, *op. cit.*, pp. 34 ff.; 152 f.

² XV, 170 f. Cf. also XI, 424: "Der erst mensch... ist aber nicht geschaffen das er also solt bleiben/ wie er anfencklich ward geschaffen/ Er war wol volkommen und auffrichtig in der Ordnung der ersten Creatur/ aber nicht inn der Ordnung der kinder Gottes/ Er war inn und zum bild und gleichnis gottes geschaffen/ Welchs auch Gott bald in jm anfieng aufzurichten/ er ist aber noch nicht Gottes bild gewest/ Sonder er solts erst kunftig durch Christum... im werck der widergeburt volkomlich werden." Cf. also XII, 87.

³ IX, 1017: "Si peccatum est accidens Quod potest in omnes homines transire ab Adam et omnes perdere...?" Cf. also VII, 805, 809, 811; XII, 601; XIII, 347. Maron, *op. cit.*, p. 29, is inaccurate in concluding. "Diese [die Sunde] wird... letztlich doch akzidentell verstanden!" Rather, in probably his only point of agreement with his opponent Flacius, Schw. asserted that sin pertained to the nature of mankind and was not accidental or peripheral to it. To be sure, sin does become *accidens* when viewed from Schw.'s concept as to what characterizes *true* humanity, for Christ became *true* man, yet remained sinless (VII, 807); believers will be without sin in the future life, but remain *true* men (VII, 305). Since the fall and in the present, however Schw. ascribed sin to the very nature of creaturely, fallen man, cf. refs. *supra*.

⁴ Cf., e.g., V, 524; VI, 617, VII, 819; XIII, 235, XIV, 450.

⁵ As noted *supra*, p 35, the relationship between sin and creaturity is very close in Schw.'s theology. While he never baldly stated that sin was a necessary attribute of creaturity, several passages besides the previous citation, VII, 547, establish potential sin as a quality of the creature, e.g., VIII, 275. "Adam hat zwar vor seinem faale Ein sundthafftig flaisch (*carnem peccabilem*) gehapt/ Nicht ein sundig oder sundtlich flaisch/ sonnder ein sundthafftig flaisch/ sag ich/ Ein flaisch dran die sund hat konden hafften." Cf. also IX, 285; XI, 235. Elsewhere

Satan were not to foil God's ultimate plan that man participate in the divine nature and thereby realize his true humanity, then a salvation process would be necessary which could deliver mankind both from the *status creaturae* as well as the *status peccati*.[1] But how was creaturely man ever to transcend his obvious creaturity? By means of the regenerating activity of God, through Christ, as *Father* rather than *Creator*! Schwenckfeld's basic dualism required – as it was occasioned by – what he termed a twofold activity on the part of God himself through the Word, in which power was succeeded by grace, the work of creation followed by that of recreation or regeneration.

> There is a vast difference between the creating office or work of God and his generating office or work. In the former God is called Creator; in the latter, Father. Cyrillus in *Thesauro Lib*: 6. Capit: 3. differentiates it in the following manner: *Creator enim ad extra producit, Genitor uero ex seipso generat* This means that God Almighty in the work of creation gives creatures their creaturely being, he also enlightens and rules them according to his will and gives to every creature, according to its nature, growth and what belongs to it. He does not, however, remain in them with his divine essence and nature, nor in the work of creation, as the heathen teach, *Iouis omnia plena* – that God is in all things essentially.
>
> But in the office or work of generation he gives his children not only being, but remains and dwells in them also with his divine essence and makes them partakers of his nature, for which reason they also are called children and new creatures This is, then, the new, gracious work, namely, the office of God's regeneration which he exercises through Christ in the Holy Spirit in all the elect, which the Scriptures call a new birth out of God from above or the rebirth....[2]

Schw. implied that *posse peccare* in the creature was itself a step in the direction of sin and imperfection, IV, 652 "Ob wol der Mensch auffrichtig in der ordnung der Creatur/ ein unschuldiges sehr gutes werck ist geschaffen/ dass er doch gegen Gotte zu achten/ nicht so gerecht/ so volkommen und unschuldig sey geschaffen.... Wa er auch dermassen mit Gottlicher gerechtigkeit/ warheit/ heiligkeit/ unnd dergleichen volkommenhait ware erschaffen/ so het er keines Gesetzes bedorfft weil dem Gerechten das Gesetz nicht wirt gegeben/ I. Timot. 1. Er het auch nicht konnen fallen noch sundigen." With much justification, therefore, Hahn, *op. cit.*, p. 8, concludes· "Schwenckfeldius contra peccati radicem non vidit in sola hominis voluntate, sed, id quod maxime proprium est ejus doctrinae, in ipsa hominis origine, quatenus non *gignendo*, sed *creando* sit ortus. Quamvis Schwenckfeldius nullo loco, quantum quidem nos scimus, hoc sibi fateatur, sequitur tamen... ex toto ejus systemate." Pietz, *op. cit.*, p. 53, similarly concludes that only Schw.'s Biblicism prevented him from frankly attributing sin to creaturity.

[1] Cf. Hahn, *op. cit* , pp. 20 f., who first clarified this point in Schw.'s theology.

It is important to note that Schw. recognizes Satan, not God, as the author of sin. Schw. was greatly offended that Zwingli, the young Luther, and Melanchthon formerly ascribed the origin of evil to God, cf. III, 23, IV, 99; XII, 942. For the origin of sin according to Schw., see also Pietz, *op. cit.*, pp. 45 ff

[2] XIV, 320 f.; cf. also II, 348, 456; III, 209; IV, 220; VI, 374, VII, 288. Regeneration is variously termed generatio, regeneratio, filiatio, Zeugung, and Wiederschopfung. Schw.'s

God's regenerating activity, thus, was effected through the person and work of the second Adam, Jesus Christ. But if the second Adam were to deliver mankind from sin and creaturity, he himself, reasoned Schwenckfeld, had to be both sinless and not a creature, even according to his humanity! It was the task of Schwenckfeldian Christology to demonstrate that, because of his origin in God's generation rather than creation, Christ was, indeed, both holy and non-creaturely. And it became the object of Schwenckfeld's soteriology to show how, by communicating his glorified flesh, Christ also enabled the believer partially to transcend sin and creaturity in this life, and fully in the life to come. For then first would man fully realize his true humanity by participating completely in the divine nature.

emphasis upon the vast conceptual difference between creation and generation was much too fundamental in his theology for such an interpretation as Schoeps', *op. cit.*, p. 34. "die Unterscheidung creare-generare ist realiter nur eine Begriffspielerei."

PART III

EXPOSITION OF SCHWENCKFELDIAN CHRISTOLOGY
AND SOTERIOLOGY

CHAPTER VIII

THE PRE-EXISTENT WORD

(1. *Die Verheissung Christi*)

Schwenckfeld entitled his doctrines concerning the person and work of Jesus *die Erkenntnis Christi*, the Knowledge of Christ.[1] According to his own classification, there are four parts to this *Erkenntnis*: 1) *die Verheissung Christi*, the promise of Christ (the pre-existent Word); 2) *die Leistung Christi*, the accomplishment of Christ (Christ in the state of humiliation); 3) *die Glorificierung Christi*, the glorification of Christ (Christ in the state of exaltation); and 4) *die Teilhaftigkeit Christi*, the participation in Christ (soteriology) (XIV, 450 ff.). This exposition will employ Schwenckfeld's systematization, discussing, in each case, first the person and then the work of Christ.

a The Person of Christ

Schwenckfeld made no significant departure from orthodox *Logos* Christology in his doctrine of the pre-existent Word. The Second Person of the Trinity [2] was begotten of the Father from eternity and served as his Agent in creating and sustaining the universe. The Word preceded the flesh with which it subsequently united, for the humanity of Jesus did not exist before his birth.[3] Indeed, so far as Christ's divine nature in general was concerned, Schwenckfeld claimed that he had no controversy with his opponents (VIII, 500). The crucial differences lay rather in the concept of Jesus' humanity.

Schwenckfeld, however, was compelled to discuss the human nature of Christ already under the category of his pre-existence because of the problem of Jesus' physical ancestry. Here he was clearly torn

---

[1] "Knowledge" only in approximate translation, for at least apprehension and understanding are also included in the pregnant German concept of Erkenntnis.

[2] Schw.'s theology is unexceptionably Trinitarian, cf. VII, 519; VIII, 347, *et passim*. Adolf Harnack, *Lehrbuch der Dogmengeschichte*, III (Freiburg i B., 1890), p. 657, misplaces Schw. in company with Valentin Weigel and Giordano Bruno among the mystic Anti-Trinitarians.

[3] Cf. Baur, *Dreieinigkeit, etc.*, pp. 248 f., for a discussion of Schw.'s differences with Andreas Osiander on this point.

between what might have been a logical consequence of his doctrine of the non-creaturity of Christ – a de-emphasis, if not a docetic denial of Jesus' genuine earthly ancestry – and the Biblical and orthodox stress on a humanity so authentic that its material origin could be traced by genealogical tables. As we shall see, Schwenckfeld maintained that Christ assumed true human flesh from the Virgin Mary, but, because of the special circumstances surrounding its conception, that flesh was non-creaturely. The problem remained, nevertheless, that the person of Mary was the product of a long, and presumably creaturely, transmission from the Old Testament patriarchs. In tracing its human ancestry through Mary to the fathers, Schwenckfeld could not tolerate the thought that the flesh of Christ should have issued from a process of mere creaturely transmission. He rather posited an explanation of Jesus' physical ancestry which is easily the least clear and satisfying theologoumenon ever propounded by the Silesian reformer.

Schwenckfeld postulated a dual line of succession from Abraham,[1] David, and the other believing fathers of Christ according to the flesh: a natural, creaturely, physical line of descent, and a spiritual succession according to the patriarchs' election, grace, and faith. Thus Abraham, for example, was a spiritual-rather than natural-forefather of Jesus:

> Abraham was not a father of Christ according to the flesh, as also the man Jesus Christ was not a physical seed of Abraham to the extent that he was born of Abraham or his fleshly descendants in the same manner as Isaac, Jacob, Judah or others.... Therefore, in the case of this promise [i.e. Jesus], a spiritual progression of the flesh of Christ is to be observed from the beginning. It is a human flesh, indeed, but the new flesh of a new man, transmitted from the holy patriarchs unto Mary after the promise in faith. According to Matthew and Luke, the bloodline of Abraham's seed through Isaac, David, and the other fathers is not ultimately directed or conducted to Christ but to Mary, through whom alone the patriarchs appertain unto Christ. Therefore Abraham, as David and others, did have some claim to the flesh of Christ, because Mary, their daughter, was a true mother of Christ the Lord.[2]

---

[1] It is significant that "believing Abraham," but never "fallen Adam," is regarded by Schw. as the forefather of Christ. In Schw.'s anthropology, Adam represented the quintessence of everything from which man had to be saved. Therefore a statement such as Schoeps', *op. cit.*, p. 29, requires modification: "Schwenckfeld will den Zusammenhang [Christi] mit der adamitischen Natur nicht zerreissen."

[2] VII, 295 f. (Cf. VII, 336, where this "claim" or "right" ceases with Christ's entry into glory.) Here Schw. enlarged on Augustine's differentiation of Christ's ancestry, *MSL* 34, 423, as cited in VII, 879: "Christus homo non latuit in materia seminis patrum sicut omnis reliqua natura humana; non decimatus est in Abraham sicut Leui." Cf. also Ambrose on a differentiated spiritual succession, *MSL* 15, 1591.

The impression is apparently conveyed that there was, indeed, a certain physical tangency between Abraham and Jesus through the person of the Virgin. In other passages Schwenckfeld also upholds the fact that Christ was born "a man of flesh, blood, soul, body, and members out of the seed of David" (VII, 303, 807). Elsewhere, however, Schwenckfeld is consistent with his thesis that a purely physical succession would predispose Jesus to creaturity and so concludes: "What the Virgin received from her fathers according to the flesh and bloodline alone did not appertain to the birth of Christ" (XII, 410). The Schwenckfeldian paradox is thus erected: Mary was a true physical descendant of Abraham, and Christ a genuine son of her flesh; yet he was not a natural, physical descendant of Abraham! Rather, an interruption occasioned by the special circumstances of Jesus' conception severed the line of physical succession, thus rendering Christ a spiritual, rather than natural or fleshly, scion of Abraham.

On the one hand, accordingly, Schwenckfeld was able to speak of a physical continuity between Abraham and Christ and a "human flesh... transmitted from the holy patriarchs" (VII, 295), and, on the other, he could emphasize the purely spiritual relationship. Schwenckfeld bridged this obvious inconsistency not only by recognizing two kinds of flesh and physical transmission – an old and a new – but also by conjoining physical and spiritual in the case of Christ! Actually, Schwenckfeld posited Jesus' ancestry as a "physico-spiritual"[1] (rather than purely spiritual) succession through the fathers. This lineage involved the transmission, within a channel separated from the natural, creaturely, sinful, fleshly succession, of a new, holy, spotless, spiritual-yet-physical flesh through the believing fathers by means of their faith in the promised Messiah and because of the determination and grace of God.[2]

---

[1] Schw. does not explicitly use this epithet, but it most aptly summarizes such frequent paradoxical associations of his as "spiritual flesh," "spiritual body," "heavenly flesh," and the like. Loetscher, *op. cit.*, 489, 494, apparently coined this compound in discussing Schw.'s theology.

[2] Cf. XIII, 10· "Also... leassen wir das fleisch Christi iuxta analogiam fide, nach der ahnlicheit des glaubens auss/ den gleubigen heiligen Vattern/ Patriarchen und Propheten seine geistliche succession oder fortgang/ biss auff Mariam/ jhre heilige Tochter/ haben/ doch dass es nicht nach dem alten sundigen fleischgange/ sonder durch einen newen sonderlichen wunderbarlichen gang der gnaden und des glaubens/ *auch leiblich*... auff Mariam die ausserwolte Mutter Christi hat gelanget/" In XIII, 17, similarly, Schw. speaks of "ein new heilig geistlich/ *auch leiblich* fleisch," which had "einen newen sonderlichen gang... allweg one sunde/ und on alle mackel...." (italics mine).

b. The Work of Christ

Clouded as Schwenckfeld's doctrine of the ancestry of Christ appears, his views on the office of the pre-existent Lord are not much clearer. With Luther he interpreted the entire Old Testament christocentrically [1] and stated that the saints under the old dispensation were saved by faith in the promised Messiah (IV, 421). But the precise nature of this faith and the problem of the patriarchs' salvation posed difficulties for Schwenckfeld which he could not always resolve consistently. At times he understood the faith of the fathers in the orthodox sense as a belief and reliance on the hidden messianic promise (*ibid.*). Schwenckfeld's fundamental soteriological principle, however, predicated salvation of a faith which apprehended the glorified flesh of Christ. But the humanity of Jesus was not, as yet, in existence, not to say glorified. Schwenckfeld met this obvious difficulty with an astonishing solution: since it existed in the prescience of God, Christ's flesh was divinely, spiritually present before the Father and could be apprehended in faith by believers even before its physical incarnation.[2] The true, living faith of the fathers invaded the eschatological realm and contemporized what lay in the future. And although Christ gained for his followers such blessings as forgiveness of sin, grace, and eternal life at a specific time, the distribution and application of these divine benefits required neither time nor place, but were made accessible to a contemporizing faith (IV, 541 ff., *et passim*). Similarly, the believing fathers in the Old Testament were truly nourished by Christ's body and blood in a spiritual Eucharist long before these physically existed.[3]

In a seemingly glaring inconsistency, however, Schwenckfeld asserted that justification and salvation did *not* immediately accompany this faith of the patriarchs.[4] The soteriological efficacy of Christ's

---

[1] IV, 429; V, 34, *et passim*.

[2] IV, 27: "Das Fleisch Christi ist wol an jm selbs noch nicht im wesen gewesen/ Es ist aber Gotte gegenwertig/ da holets auch der glaube."

[3] IV, 27: "Die speisung ist vor Gott ausser aller zeit unnd stehet in coelestibus, unnd geschücht allhie allein durch einen waren lebendigen glauben/ Wer nun die art und Natur des glaubens hat erkant/ der weiss dass jm alle künfftige unnd vergangne ding eben als wol als Gotte gegenwertig sind... wiewol es vor unns dort im alten Testament noch zukünfftig war/ so war es doch den Gleubigen warhafftig im glauben gegenwertig." From this contemporizing concept of faith and its definition as the believer's apprehension of the flesh of Christ should be viewed Schw.'s unusual theologoumenon concerning the physico-spiritual transmission of Christ's humanity by the believing fathers, cf. VIII, 855. In other words, Schw. understood the patriarchs as ancestors of the humanity of Jesus primarily because they carried him, through faith, in their hearts rather than in their loins.

[4] In IV, 530, he concluded that "keine ware gerechtigkeit/ keine gnad/ kein heiliger Geist vor dem verdienst des leidens Christi offenbarlich in der Kirchen der Juden sein mochte/

glorified flesh, otherwise independent of time, was, indeed, confined to a specific point of time in the case of the believing fathers. Their redemption was first achieved during the victorious descent of Jesus into hell! For Schwenckfeld did not jettison the inherited medieval doctrine of the *limbus patrum*, although logically it had no place in his system. Rather, he asserted that before the glorified Lord triumphed over Satan, stormed the gates of hell, and released the spirits imprisoned there, no one gained salvation or entered heaven (IV, 522, 525-53). All the holy patriarchs and prophets hoped and waited for Christ's redemption in limbo, which Schwenckfeld also termed the "suburbs [or outpost – *Vorburg*] of hell," and the "bosom of Abraham."[1] Their condition, however, was painless and did not resemble that of the godless damned. Jesus emptied this prison after his victory over Satan and took the souls of the saints with him to heaven, where the spirits of all the saved proceed immediately after death since that time.[2] If Schwenckfeld's retention of the *limbus patrum* did logically follow upon his doctrine of the soteriological indispensability of Christ's humanity, which was essentially nonexistent before the Incarnation, it nevertheless belied his concept of faith as contemporizing its object, the glorified flesh of Christ. For if faith actually "makes all future things present,"[3] if it truly substantializes what is hoped for, the future humanity of the *Logos* and therefore redemption, as heaven itself, should have been appropriated by the believing fathers in their day. Schwenckfeld's inconsistency in this regard is best explained by the fact that he considered Christ's triumph over Satan as a primary redemptive mode, although *Christus Victor* otherwise played only a relatively minor role in his system, as we shall see. Moreover, Schwenckfeld generally regarded the person and work of the promised Messiah as only a special problem in his theology.

sondern... alles unterm Gesetz/ unterm unglauben/ unnd unter der sunden noch ist beschlossen gewesen/ unnd beschlossen blieben muste/ biss dass Christus der samen Abrahe/ ...das fleisch durch sein leiden und sterben erlosete." Cf. also IV, 523, 529.

[1] *Loc. cit.* Despite a perceptive discussion of the problem, Loetscher, *op. cit.*, 493, implies that the concept of the *limbus patrum* is exceptional in Schw. Nowhere, however, did Schw. explicitly state that the fathers were in heaven before Christ, and the notion of the *limbus* remained consistent in his theology, cf. IV, 523; V, 421; X, 363, *et passim*.

[2] IV, 522 f., 543, 545; V, 421; X, 363. Planck, *op. cit.*, p. 119, probably considering only the passage in IV, 523, asserts that Schw. denied salvation for the Old Testament fathers. Cf. also Charles Hodge, *Systematic Theology*, II (London, 1871), 587.

[3] IV, 541: "...der lebendige ware glaub... alle zukunfftige ding gegenwertig machet."

CHAPTER IX

CHRIST IN THE STATE OF HUMILIATION

(2. *Die Leistung Christi*)

a. The Person of Christ

Schwenckfeld's motivations in denying the creaturity of Jesus first in the state of exaltation and then also in the humiliation have been discussed. Early in the christological controversy, Schwenckfeld drew up a manifesto of fourteen arguments which propounded the theological necessity of Christ's non-creaturity.[1] Following is a summary of these propositions which find frequent repetition in his christological treatises:

1) If Christ the man were a creature, heavenly or earthly, he could not be the true, natural son of God according to his entire person.

2) The knowledge of Christ, indeed Christ himself could not be eternal life if, because of a creaturely flesh, he were today circumscribed spatially and temporally. He would be the object of reason, not faith.

3) Faith in Jesus would be false and divided if he had a creaturely admixture, for faith cannot have its object both in God and the creature, heavenly or earthly.

4) If Christ's were a creaturely humanity, he could not be the head of the church, which is his body, nor our high priest, intermediary, and king sitting at the right hand of God. A creature cannot rule with God nor be his equal.

5) The one, simple person of Jesus would be divided His humanity would either be subjected to the Godhead or would constitute the fourth person in the essence of God.

6) The whole Jesus Christ, God and man, could not dwell in the hearts of believers, since the human heart is incapable of receiving a creature. Therefore only a half-Christ would inhabit the heart.

"Was fur Irrung/ Abfal/ von Christo und ungeschuckligkeit uss der leer folget/ die Christum den menschen nun fur ein Creatur helt" (1538), VI, 86 ff. These fourteen arguments are repeated in modified form in subsequent treatises, cf. VI, 128 ff., 534 ff.; XIV, 496 ff. Although most of the theses refer to Christ's office in the state of exaltation – this was the coign of vantage for Schw.'s entire theology – he also concluded that Creator and creature were mutually intolerable in one Lord even in humiliation, cf. *supra*.

7) Jesus the man could not be the foundation and cornerstone upon which the temple of God is constructed. God would never use a creature for this purpose.

8) If Christ's were a creaturely humanity, his body could not be a life-giving flesh nor a true food for the soul. What, then, would be the significance of the Lord's Supper?

9) Similarly, the blood of Jesus could not be a true drink for the soul.

10) Were he a creature, the man, Jesus Christ, could not be the future judge.

11) Christ would be capable of nothing more than Moses, Peter, Paul, or any other saint or prophet in heaven. He would be a higher creature and occupy a more exalted position than the rest, but he could not administer his present, Scriptural offices in our behalf.

12) He could not be the seed of blessing from which the children of God are reborn. He could neither bless, free, nor sanctify us, since God alone is so capable.

13) The body of Christ would not be a body of heavenly clarity, nor the dwelling place of the whole fullness of Deity.

14) The believer would be compelled to have faith in, pray to, and worship a half-Christ as God and Lord, since one may not accord a creature such divine honor.

In fine, God had concentrated his entire soteriological activity in the humanity of Christ. By reason of its origin, past accomplishment, and present nature and office of saving mankind from sin and creaturity, that humanity was necessarily non-creaturely.

Proceeding from the soteriological necessity of Jesus' non-creaturity and glory, Schwenckfeld also developed arguments in support of the same from the nature of Christ's person. He devoted much attention to the doctrine of the Incarnation, for here his theology was particularly vulnerable, and yet, as Schwenckfeld insisted, defensible in view of the special circumstances under which the Word became flesh. His opponents, especially the Swiss, repeatedly insisted that if the humanity of Christ had a beginning and consisted in true, human flesh, then that humanity was creaturely. Schwenckfeld wrote treatise after treatise granting the premises but rejecting the conclusion. Although he considered it his opponents' most potent argument, the lay reformer denied that everything which had a beginning was either a creature or something created (XI, 358). Only philosophers would make such a proposition. Theologians, on the other hand, could recognize two kinds of origins in the cosmos: the creaturely, issuing from God's creative activity; and a new, divine, spiritual derivation, proceeding from the generative activity of God as Father, not Creator. Of the latter, Christ was the eminent example. Schwenckfeld applied the "begotten, not made" of the Nicean formula to the whole Lord, not only to the divine nature or eternal *Logos*. He also listed such other originations in divine generation rather than creation as the celestial Jerusalem, the new heaven, the new earth, justifying faith, and the like (VIII, 378; XI, 358). Similarly Schwenckfeld countered the argument that the genuine human flesh of Jesus necessarily presupposed creaturity. Again, corresponding to the twofold activity of God as Creator or Father, he posited two Adams, two types of flesh, two kinds of humanity: creaturely man; and new, spiritual, non-creaturely man (VI, 236, *et passim*). Such a dichotomy, however, necessarily made of "man" a generic concept and of "creature" a specific. Schwenckfeld did, in fact, assert that the designation "creature" was not an essential characteristic of humanity! Creaturity did not pertain to the substance of man, but was an *accidens* referring to human origins and similar to the terms "birth," "sonship," and "regeneration."[1] On the other hand, the possession of flesh, blood, and members, body and soul belonged to the true substance of man, characterizing both the non-creaturely Christ and the very creaturely sinner (VII, 247).

In his doctrine of the Incarnation, Schwenckfeld pointed up the unique significance of the Virgin Birth in the determination of Jesus' humanity. Quite naturally the role of the divine rather than the human was stressed. God and Mary were far from coordinates in generating Jesus, and Christ was not simply half son of God and half son of the Virgin in the sense that the divine nature came from God, and the human nature from Mary (VII, 299). Repeatedly Schwenck-

---

[1] VII, 563. "Creatura non est nomen substantie rei sed appellatio rei accidens, sicut natiuitas, sicut filiatio, generatio &c." Schw. cites Ambrose as accounting creaturity an *accidens*, cf. *MSL*, 16, 842. It is curious that Schw. should consider sin a substantial part of humanity when he regarded creaturity as only accidental to mankind. While creaturity involves "grosser underscheid" between Christ and the rest of humanity, XIII, 346, it is sin which involves the essential difference, cf. VII, 805, *et supra*. Indeed, in some passages Schw. cites sin as the only fundamental difference, e.g., V, 522; IX, 983 ff. This lends weight to the inference that Schw.'s aversion for the term "creature" stems ultimately from his associating creaturity with sin, cf. *supra*, p. 42.

Whether, in terms of his system, Schw. could justifiably regard creaturity as accidental to man is questionable. If creaturity were only an *accidens* of humanity, why should Schw. have staked his Christology and soteriology to the necessity of Christ's *non*-creaturity? Obviously creaturity involved something substantial in his theology. The dualism in God's creating and generating activities was too profound in Schw.'s thought to be interpreted in any accidental sense. His resort to explaining creaturity as *accidens*, therefore, was clearly guided by apologetic necessities rather than the logic of his system.

feld maintained against the Swiss that God was the true, *natural* father not only of the Word, but of Jesus' humanity as well! Therefore the human nature of Christ participated in divinity not only out of union with the Word, but because God was the genuine father also of that humanity.

> The man Christ... did not participate in the essence and nature of divinity only by reason of union with the Word... but because he himself, also according to his flesh, body, and soul was divinely adorned and made glorious and rich by birth from God his father. He brought this all with him naturally and hereditarily at the beginning of his deification and from the first moment of his conception; wherein he then grew and increased before God and man unto complete perfection, when the man, Jesus Christ, became God in and with God his father and completely possessed and assumed the divine nature in heaven [1]

In emphasizing that Christ the man was the *natural* son of God (II, 520; VII, 334), Schwenckfeld opposed the teaching of the "Nestorians, Adoptionists, and Creaturists [*Creaturisten*]" that the humanity of Jesus was God's son by adoption, or, as the Arian *nuncupatione*, "in name only" (VII, 327).

A further example of Schwenckfeld's stress on the role of the divine in the Incarnation is his singular notion concerning the *origin* of Christ's flesh, which he ascribed to God the Father rather than jointly to God and the Virgin Mary. Probably assuming that God in the Holy Spirit was the efficient cause of Jesus' conception, Schwenckfeld wrote: "It is true that the origin of such a flesh did not derive from Mary, as, indeed, in otherwise common birth the origin of the child is usually attributed not to the mother but to the father."[2] In one excerpt Schwenckfeld even stated that from the point of view of fatherhood, source, and origin "... both natures, each according to its condition and property, come from God" (VII, 334). Other passages also betray crypto-docetic tendencies in his Christology: "The man in Christ shared in divinity not only because of union with the Word, but also himself shortly after [*bald nach*] his conception brought something with him as his own possession from his father which is of God and divine."[3] In a particularly unguarded moment,

---

[1] VII, 328 f.; cf. also III, 558; VII, 299 f., 336.

[2] VII, 324; cf. also VII, 300, 304, 540 ff. Schw. cited Hilary as ascribing the origin of Christ's flesh to God while upholding the true motherhood of Mary, cf. *MSL* 10, 354 f.

[3] VII, 734; cf. also VII, 328 f. Similarly VIII, 782 Christ's flesh "... bald vom empfengknus an/ etwas Gotlichs und des was Gott ist naturlich gehabt/ und darinn zur volle Gottes ist gewachsen/" Exactly what this "something" was is never precisely defined by Schw. It should probably be understood as that divine seed or potential within Christ's humanity which would effect its progressive growth in deity, cf. *infra*.

Schwenckfeld could even make the exceptional statement: "...I know that Christ was conceived by the Holy Spirit in heaven." [1]

The reformer tried to preserve his Christology from such apparent Docetism by his teaching concerning the role of Mary in the Incarnation and a parallel stress on the true humanity of Christ. Because he had to explain in some manner how the Virgin could be a creature and yet conceive a non-creature, why she could be a descendant of sinful flesh and still give birth to holy flesh, and by what means she could separate the humanity of Christ from its ancestry in point of creaturity and sin – Schwenckfeld's Mariology is necessarily involved. Against charges of Docetism he emphasized the true humanity of Jesus, beginning with the fact that the Virgin Mary was the true and natural mother of Christ (VII, 319). The Word assumed genuine human flesh directly from her and from no other source or substance.[2] Despite the special nature of Christ's conception, the maternal functions remained natural and the child developed and was born in normal fashion, but with no harm to Mary (VII, 324; IX, 799). Rejected were such dilutions as would make of the mother's role a mere *productio, transitio*, or a preternatural parturition (*ibid.*; VII, 103). When the Word became flesh a true conception took place, not merely the "reception" by Mary of a Word which already previously had assumed flesh.[3] The

---

[1] VII, 807. Statements such as these probably led Baur, *Dreieinigkeit, etc.*, p. 236, to conclude "...behauptet auch Schwenckfeld keine eigentliche Geburt aus der Maria.... Christus ist daher nicht sowohl aus der Maria, als vielmehr in ihr geboren. Seinem substanziellen Ursprung nach hat demnach Christus nichts aus der Maria, was er Menschliches an sich hat, gehort also nur der Erscheinung an." While a few of Schw's statements, if isolated, would seem to indicate such conclusions, his anti-docetic asseverations in the following discussion directly contradict Baur's assertions. When Schw. speaks of the origin of Christ's humanity in God, this is to be understood in a causational and efficient sense.

A certain ambivalence in Schw.'s doctrine of the Incarnation is, however, undeniable. On the one hand was his natural inclination to insure the non-creaturely and sinless nature of his Lord's flesh by ascribing to it a totally divine origin. On the other hand, the reality of Jesus' physical humanity dared not be denied, his bond with the rest of mankind dared not be too grossly severed or Christ could not remain the Savior of humanity. Accordingly, Schw. sought also to uphold the fleshly continuity between true mother and true son.

[2] IX, 799. "ex visceribus maternis." Cf. VII, 310: "...das Fleisch Christi der Substantz/ Materi oder Natur Marie [ist] gewest/ und dass Gott sein Menscheit nicht anderswoher/ weder auss Marien der Junckfrawen... an sich genommen/ und also warhafftig Mensch sey worden." Cf. also VI, 238.

[3] IX, 799. "Maria hat nicht das Wort/ das on jr zuthun ware Fleisch worden/ erst darnach empfangen/ sondern das Wort ist im empfencknis Fleisch worden." This against the doctrine of Melchior Hoffman, *vide infra*. Cf. also VII, 319; IX, 814.

relationship between God and the Virgin Mary is expressed: "God the Father is the author and producer in his Spirit. Mary is the manufactory [*officina*] and provides the flesh" (IX, 800).

As to the moment of Incarnation:

> Indeed, as soon as Mary believed the message of the angel, the Word became flesh and Christ, God and man, was conceived in her instantaneously.... Briefly, God the heavenly Father sent out his Word and, in addition, the Holy Spirit for the construction of the temple of Jesus Christ... In Mary he found, so to say, the green wood and precious material for this construction, that is, a clean, holy flesh born out of God; and from this he took, in quick mastery, what and how much he wished.[1]

But the Virgin's "clean, holy flesh, born out of God" posed a decided problem in Schwenckfeldian Mariology. For if that part of Mary's humanity which was conceived by the Holy Spirit to generate Christ were sinless and non-creaturely, what of the rest of her body? Although Schwenckfeld's understanding of the divine role in the Incarnation might have been sufficient to account for the differentiation between that part of the Virgin's humanity which was assumed by the Word and the rest of her person, he soon arrived at conclusions which, he thought, would the better shield his crusading concerns: like Christ's, the flesh of Mary was also sinless! Since God has no fellowship with the unrighteous, the Holy Infant could not be nourished in her body next to sinful flesh (XII, 613). Rather, "...it must be a new woman with a new material and renewed flesh, the same, indeed, as other women so far as the nature is concerned, but very different in regard to her sanctification. She can no longer have any sinful flesh in her, nor be subject to sin like other women, but is sanctified by God above all other women" (XII, 603).

Mary was especially chosen by the Almighty before the foundation of the world to be holy and irreproachable in his sight.[2] From her childhood she was preserved by God from sin (XI, 767). She also remained *semper virgo* (XII, 604). The fact that Mary was not entirely free from human affections and desires and could not

---

[1] VII, 321. The faith of Mary is thus accorded an instrumental significance in the conception of Christ. Cf. also VII, 551 "Der glaub jnn Maria had diss kindt vom H. gaiste empfangen;" and VII, 557. The implications of these statements will better be understood in connection with Schw.'s substantial concept of faith, *vide infra*, ch. XI.

[2] VII, 312. Cf. also IX, 778. In IX, 799, the body of Mary consists of "...heilig/ keusch reine fleisch/ welchs auch zuuor in jhr durchs Wort war erzeuget/" Elsewhere Schw. implies that the holiness was only contemporaneous with the conception of Christ, e.g., XII, 603. "...das weib hat ihr heiligkeit auss gnaden vom samen Christo Ihrem Sohn empfangen/"

always discern the will of God did not detract from her holiness.[1]

In this manner Schwenckfeld disposed of the problem of sin in his Mariology, but what of the question of creaturity? He did not undertake the bizarre by attempting to deny the creaturity of Mary. She was, indeed, a creature (IX, 801), but a holy "new creature" (IX, 1009) and more highly sanctified than the Pauline regenerate (XII, 602). Yet she could not transmit creaturity to her offspring: "For although the mother of Christ was a creature, she did not conceive her child Jesus from any creature. She also did not bear him according to the course and order of creatures."[2] Moreover there was a basic difference between the humanity of Mary and that of her son, despite elements of physical continuity.

> Although they, the same as far as the substance is concerned, are both flesh, Mary's is a sanctified flesh from the succession of the fathers. But the humanity of Christ does not derive from the succession of the fathers, but is a promised, holy flesh, new by nature. Therefore it could not see decay nor remain in death.[3]

Schwenckfeld's crusading doctrines of the non-creaturity and glorification of Christ's humanity obviously exposed him to charges of heresy, and his opponents variously classified him among the Docetists, Eutychians, Origenists, Valentinians, Sabellians, Marcionites, Samosatians, Manichaeists, Timothiani, Apollinarists, Cerdonists, and Hoffmanites. Schwenckfeld, however, roundly condemned all these as errorists.[4] He took pains to emphasize the true humanity of

---

[1] The doctrine of the immaculate conception of Mary would seem logically to follow such a view of the Virgin's holiness. At first Schw. considered the theologoumenon a mere "monkish disputation" arising from a creaturely conception of Christ's origin (VII, 322, 535). Later, however, he doubtless implicitly accepted the immaculate conception when, referring again to the controversy, he asserted that the Virgin was not under the curse of original sin, XI, 768: "Wir wellen auch nit sagen/ das Maria darfür ehe sie Christum empfangen/ sowol als andere menschen unterm fluche gewest ist/ das wellen wir nicht halten/" In later years, however, there was some modification in Schw.'s Mariology. Again he distinguished between an old and a new nature in the Virgin: the old, as she was a descendant of Adam and Eve, the daughter of Joachim and Anna; and the new, as she was the elect, holy, believing Virgin, full of grace, who gave birth to Christ (XIV, 844). Cf. also V, 487. Significant, moreover, is the fact that Schw. and Crautwald never ascribed any soteriological function to Mary. All maternal rights and prerogatives over her son ended with his death on the cross. After his glorification, Christ was son only of God (V, 487; VI, 256). Mary was not bodily assumed into heaven; nor does she intercede for the believer (XIV, 881).

[2] IX, 801; cf. also VII, 877.

[3] XII, 617; cf. also XIV, 844 f. "Succession" here must be understood as a purely "fleshly succession," or we find a discrepancy between this and earlier views, cf. VII, 303, 807.

[4] Cf. VII, 306, 316, 325, 520, 590; IX, 776-68, 792, 810.

Jesus not only by not etherializing the relationship between Christ and his mother in the Incarnation, but also in attacking any position which would compromise the physical reality of Jesus' flesh in the state of humiliation. Against the Hoffmanites Schwenckfeld insisted that Christ did not bring his flesh with him from heaven, but assumed it from the Virgin Mary.[1] He did, however, admit: "Both of them [Melchior Hoffman and Sebastian Franck] sucked their error out of our truth, as the spider sucks poison out of a precious flower. God have mercy on them and us."[2] Similarly, Schwenckfeld asserted that Christ should not even be termed "a heavenly man" in the sense that his flesh came from heaven (IX, 817). He had no chimerical body (*phantastischen Leib*, IX, 778), but flesh which was visible, passible, and mortal.

The touchstone of Schwenckfeld's sincerity regarding the genuine humanity of Jesus is finally the question of the relationship between Christ's flesh and that of mankind in general. On the one hand, he emphasized the soteriological necessity that Jesus assume "our flesh." "Otherwise how could our flesh come to heaven and have fellowship with God...?" (IV, 113). "Certainly it is also a comfort for us above every comfort that in Christ our nature now sits in heavenly being, reigns, and represents us continually "(V, 521). Similarly, Jesus is

---

[1] VI, 237-78; IX, 778. J. L. Neve and O. W. Heick, *A History of Christian Thought*, II (Philadelphia, 1946), 42, are mistaken in this regard "Christ's body, in its flesh and blood, was not from Mary, but from God. He brought it with him from heaven." Similarly Hodge, *op. cit.*, I, 82. "His body and soul were formed out of the substance of God." Cf. also Planck, *op. cit.*, pp. 148 ff.

[2] V, 522 f.; cf. also VI, 237. As Hirsch, *op. cit.*, pp. 167 f., and Schoeps, *op. cit.*, pp. 28-31, have observed, the relationship between Schw. and Melchior Hoffman was important for the development of Schw.'s Christology and Mariology. Not a few of his christological treatises were evoked in opposition to Hoffman's teaching, which, in ascribing – like Schw. – a heavenly *origin* to the flesh of Jesus, nevertheless denied the true motherhood of Mary. Schw., however, traced the flesh of Christ precisely to the Virgin Birth, the special circumstances of which provided him with a solution to the problem of maintaining Jesus' connection with mankind while upholding his sinlessness and non-creaturity. Hoffman, on the other hand, in identifying all earthly flesh – including Mary's – with sin, felt compelled to sunder the heavenly flesh of Christ from all terrestrial humanity. Accordingly, Schw. charged him with Valentinian Christology, cf. IV, 113, 835; V, 486, 521; VI, 122 ff., 237 ff., 482, 513; and IX, 794.

Schw. and Hoffman were personally acquainted with each other. Both arrived in Strassburg in 1529, and Schw. visited the Anabaptist after he had been cast into prison by the city authorities for his unorthodox views. Schw. opposed the imprisonment and defended those aspects of Hoffman's doctrine which coincided with his, i.e., the emphasis on the glorified humanity of Christ, and the use of John six as a hermeneutical key in the interpretation of the Eucharist. Schw. also tried to convince the Anabaptist of what he considered his major error, the denial that Christ assumed true human flesh from the Virgin Mary (IV, 835). Cf. F. O. zur Linden, *Melchior Hofmann* (Haarlem, 1885), pp. 187 ff.; 320 ff.

designated "our Brother" (V, 783; IX, 198). Yet Schwenckfeld also stressed the fundamental differences between Brother and brother. Christ had a nature nobler than the rest of humanity (VII, 313). He was the "highest man," "the fairest of all men" (XIII, 347). Not only did he receive from God the Father at birth such divine qualities as "... holiness, grace, righteousness, the Holy Spirit, newness, truth, etc.," [1] but in certain fundamental respects he differed from mankind even before the fall. Jesus was sinless, unable to sin (VIII, 274), and, by reason of his total natural sonship from the Father, not a creature (VII, 539, *et passim*). And precisely because of these cardinal differences from the rest of mankind, the humanity of Christ could realize full participation in the divine nature. Schwenckfeld therefore concluded that the flesh of Jesus was and was not ours (V, 522; VII, 539). The Son of God was and was not our Brother (V, 521, 783; VII, 814). In this identity and in this difference lay the possibility that Christ could be the Savior of mankind.

Schwenckfeld's understanding of the relationship between the divine and the human natures in Jesus upheld the Chalcedonian formula of two natures in one personal union (III, 387), but his real sympathies lay with Ephesus (VIII, 520). The earliest purely christological statements of Schwenckfeld voiced objection to the division of Christ's person by some of his contemporaries (II, 351-57), and a predominant feature in his system continued to be a heavy stress on the unity in the person of Jesus. In this respect, Schwenckfeld's entire Christology may be understood as a protest against the Nestorianizing tendencies of Swiss theology in favor of a near-Eutychian emphasis which approximated many elements in Luther's Christology.[2] At the

---

[1] XI, 270. Significantly, Schw. regarded these not as mere attributes, "*accidentia*, zufellige ding," but "*merae substantiae*, eitel selbstendig wesen" (XIII, 347).

[2] The relationship between the Christologies of Luther and Schw. have variously been appraised. On the one hand, Hirsch, *op. cit.*, p. 165, states: "Schwenckfelds Christologie, wie wir sie kennen, ist doch nur eine Spielart der lutherischen." So also Dorner, *Entwicklungsgeschichte, etc.*, pp. 575-77 "Unter der namhafteren reformatorischen Mannern hat mit Luthers christologischer Grundanschauung ohne Zweifel keiner mehr aehnlichkeit, als Andreas Osiander und unter denen, die sich ausserhalb der kirchlichen Bewegung hielten, der vielverkannte C. Schwenckfeld." Cf. also Schultz, *op. cit.*, p. 291. *Per contra* Maron, *op. cit.*, p. 174 (referring to Christology), states: "...hat er [Schw] doch in Wahrheit mit Luther nichts gemein." The latter judgement is too extreme and evaluates Schw's Christology only through his anthropology and soteriology, which, it is true, differed completely from that of Luther. However, so far as the doctrine of the person of Christ *per se* is concerned, Schw. and Luther were very much closer. Luther's quasi-Alexandrian views are common knowledge, and his doctrine of the ubiquity of Christ's body was but the logical consequence of Schw.'s own Christology. In several letters Luther also refrained from calling Christ a creature, cf. Schw.'s citation of these in VI, 541;

beginning of his controversy with the Silesian theologian, Vadian had sounded the keynote: if Schwenckfeldian Christology were correct, then Eutyches had been unjustly anathematized by the church. This evoked Schwenckfeld's rejoinder: if Vadian were correct, then Nestorius had been falsely condemned (VII, 698). The greater portion of Schwenckfeld's massive *Confession* is devoted to excoriating "modern Swiss Nestorians" [1] who would make two persons out of the one Lord. According to Schwenckfeld, they dichotomized Christ's person and office both in the states of humiliation and exaltation as follows:

> Christ, only according to one nature without the other –
> Is the true son of God
> Has God as father
> Was conceived by the Holy Ghost.
> Was born of the Virgin Mary.
> Suffered and died on the cross.
> Is the head and foundation of the church.
> Dwells in the members of his body.
> Is the life-giving food for the soul.
> Is our mediator and high priest.
> Makes righteous and blessed.
> Is the second person of the Trinity.
> Is the essence of the Holy Trinity.
> Is equal to his father in power, honor, and glory.
> Forgives sins and sends the Holy Spirit.
> Is to be worshipped
> Is Lord and God (VIII, 563 f).

The Swiss, he felt, could not salvage the unity in Christ by means of their *communicatio idiomatum*. In fact, Schwenckfeld posited a union so close that he dismissed the "sophistic *communicatio*" as a norm for the relationship between the human and divine natures in

---

VIII, 686, 712 f. Cf. also E. L. Enders, *Dr. Martin Luthers Briefwechsel* (Frankfurt a. M., 1884 ff.), XV, 250. We must not, however, overlook the significant differences between Lutheran and Schwenckfeldian Christology. These include Luther's acceptance of the *communicatio idiomatum*; his doctrine of ubiquity; much of the Christology of the Incarnation, particularly the ancestry of Jesus, and, of course, the nature and function of the indwelling Christ.

Schw. claimed that Luther, Melanchthon, and Brentz also originally taught a *Gottwerdung* of Christ's humanity. For his summary of christological statements by the Wittenbergians which, he contended, corresponded to his, see VIII, 689 ff. This reference is a letter to Luther, dated Oct. 12, 1543, in which Schw. made a final attempt to conciliate the reformer by pointing out the similarities in their Christologies. For Luther's famous, uncivil reply, see VIII, 719-20, and Enders, *op. cit.*, p. 276.

[1] IV, 19; VIII, 515 ff. is Schw.'s most systematic critique of Nestorius.

Christ.[1] Nor did he hesitate to underscore the intimacy of the *unio personalis* by hailing the Virgin Mary as θεοτόκος (VIII, 520), asserting that in Christ God truly suffered and died,[2] and arguing, "if, then, the eternal God can be born, undoubtedly he can also suffer" (V, 752).

> Christ, the Son of God, the whole person, God and man entirely, that is, unitedly was given into death and died. One nature did not die without the other, just as one did not suffer without the other, so little as one is without the other. The suffering and death of Christ pertained not only to his humanity – just as now his glory is not limited only to his divinity – but to God and man, the entire Son of God in the united person who hung on the cross and died (V, 648).

Schwenckfeld feared that any tendency to preserve the honor of God against birth, suffering, and death by restricting these functions to Jesus' humanity in the state of humiliation would be complemented by a virtual exclusion of that humanity from the full glorification, deification, and prerogatives due it in the state of exaltation. And it cannot sufficiently be emphasized that the ultimate heresy according to Schwenckfeld's theology – he himself equated it with the sin against the Holy Ghost (VIII, 751) – was to detract from the present glory of Christ's humanity by imposing upon it creaturely limitations and abridging its functions. Accordingly, Schwenckfeld emphasized that the genuine unity of the divine and human natures in Jesus extended over both the states of humiliation and exaltation; or, as he phrased it, the divine mysteries of the birth, suffering, and glory of Christ apply to the whole, undivided Lord (VII, 609). For if the *unio personalis* were in any way jeopardized during the state of humiliation, it might also be compromised in the exaltation, and Schwenckfeld wanted a "half-Christ" in neither state (V, 648, 743). Consequently, in stressing the totality of the personal union, he could say: "They [the natures], however, are joined in a unity so nearly inexpressible that reason cannot grasp them as unmixed... only faith can properly distinguish the *Verbum caro factum est*, as also the man now in the essence of God" (VII, 673).

"Mixture," in fact, is precisely the term Schwenckfeld's opponents used in criticizing his Christology, particularly the emphasis on an even closer union of Jesus' natures in the state of glorification. Both in his own day and since, no single charge was levelled more repeatedly

---

[1] VII, 591; cf. also VIII, 526: "...es ist noch ein ander vil subtiler Teilung mit der *Communicatio idomatum/* von den ungleubigen Sophisten/ Christo und seiner gantzheit zur schmach erdacht worden/"

[2] II, 357; IV, 793; V, 648; VII, 698, 701.

against Schwenckfeld than that of Eutychianism or monophysitism.¹ He was very sensitive to these accusations and countered by rejecting "heretic Eutyches" and his monophysitic vitiation of Christ's true humanity (VII, 287). Together with the Valentinian denial that Jesus assumed true flesh from Mary, Schwenckfeld even asserted that the teaching of Eutyches was a "much more dangerous error" than the Nestorian division of Christ!² Similarly, he rejected the Christology of the Timothiani,³ who regarded the natures of Christ as mixed or blended, and that of the Apollinarists, who held that the natures were suspended in a fusion of the divine and human.⁴

Schwenckfeld's systematic explanation of the Incarnation did not posit a mixture of the two natures in Christ, nor a fusion or transformation (*Verwandlung*) of the Word into flesh: "I say, then, that the Word became flesh, and God man not by conversion, through metamorphosis, also not by transformation, through alteration or mutation, transfiguration, annihilation, or extinction... but by assumption, conjunction, union, through reception, amalgamation...."⁵

Probably as a concession to orthodoxy, Schwenckfeld did, indeed, differentiate the natures in Christ to some extent, but only in so far as the unity of his person were not jeopardized:

¹ E.g., Planck, *op. cit.*, p. 120, asserts that Schw.'s concept of the deified humanity of Christ approximated "...die alte Haupt-Ketzerey des schon im funften Jahrhundert verdammten Eutyches...." Cf. also a modern textbook: F. E. Mayer, *The Religious Bodies of America* (St. Louis, 1954), p. 416: "This [Schw.'s] theory of a complete deification of Christ's human nature is the most complete form of Eutychian monophysitism." *Per contra*-Hahn, *op. cit.*, p. 76· "Caspar Schwenckfeldius neque Docetismi neque Eutychianismi jure potest accusari." Cf. Erbkam, *op. cit.*, p. 467. Dorner, *op cit.*, p. 635, also defends Schw. against the charge of Eutychianism: "...Schwenckfelds Christologie gar nicht die Geringschatzung verdient, die ihr so lange Zeit hindurch zu Theil geworden ist. Ebenso wenig darf sie mit dem Eutychianismus gleichgesetzt werden." Baur, "Mystik, etc.," pp. 519 f., is not as prepared fully to absolve Schw. of the charge of Eutychianism, because he feels that the true humanity of Christ is compromised in his Christology. Most charges of Eutychianism refer especially to Schw.'s Christology of the state of exaltation, see *infra*.

² IX, 812; cf. also VI, 580; VII, 330, 521.

³ After Timotheus Aelurus, bishop of Alexandria in the fifth century; VII, 520.

⁴ *Loc. cit.* Cf., however, Baur, *op. cit.*, pp. 527 f.: "...unter den altern Christologen keiner grössere Aehnlichkeit mit Schwenckfeld hat, als Apollinaris. Beide haben dasselbe Interesse, die Einheit des Gottmenschen festzuhalten.... die Christologie des Apollinaris hat hierin etwas Mystisches, das Verhältniss Christi zu dem Glaubigen aber fasste er nicht mystisch, wie Schwenckfeld, sondern moralisch auf."

⁵ IX, 812: "Also sage ich ist das Wort Fleisch/ und Gott mensch worden/ nicht conuersione, durch verwandlung/ auch nicht transformatione, durch venderung/ weder mutatione, vergestaltung/ noch peremptione, abtilgung... Sondern Assumptione, coniunctione, vnitione, durch annemmung/ vereinigung/.." In IX, 802, the Word becomes flesh through "annemmung... vereinigung/ zufügung/ einwonunge/ bekleidung rc." Cf. also VII, 310.

Particularly in the state of humiliation may one consider the properties of each nature, distinguish them properly – distinguish, I say, not divide – and observe the qualities of each, so that the natures remain entire; for... Jesus was not yet glorified Nor was the almighty Word of God limited to the humanity of Christ. Therefore it is permissible *Quid cuiusque naturae respectu dicatur*, but only in such a manner as before observed, and as the dear fathers did it, namely, that thereby Christ, the only Son of God, be maintained entire by faith.[1]

The properties of humanity and divinity, however, although themselves distinguishable, were not to be separated in the activities of Christ, for none of these took place without the participation of both natures.[2] Consequently Schwenckfeld rejected such expressions as: "the whole Christ sleeps, but according to the human nature; the whole Christ commands the wind and the waves, but according to the divine nature" (VII, 663). Rather the same Jesus, God-man, θεάνθρωπος does everything "wholly and unitedly" (*ibid.*).

At one point in Christ's existence, however, Schwenckfeld was compelled to acknowledge that the natures were separated, if only temporarily. The death of Jesus involved a dissolution of the *unio personalis* in which the body was buried, but the soul, remaining united with the divine Word, descended into hell, triumphed over Satan, and was reunited with the body in the resurrection (VII, 636, 708). Later, however, Schwenckfeld sought to retrieve unity even in Christ's death by stating that since the soul is part of humanity, indeed, *potissima humanitatis pars*, the divine and human natures were never entirely separated, for the soul remained united with the Word (IX, 685 ff.).

Just as the human nature of Christ introduces the major christological problem in the state of exaltation, so the divine nature poses the chief difficulty in the humiliation. In the interests of profoundest unity, one solution is a kenosis in the nineteenth-century sense of a self-depotentialization of the *Logos*, and there are several passages in Schwenckfeld's writings which have a kenotic ring in this interpretation:

[1] VII, 650. Schw. also differentiated between a divine and a human will in Christ and rejected Vadian's charge that he was a monothelitist. Cf. VII, 701: "Sonst das Christus inn der dispensation zwen ungleiche (nicht widerwertige) willen gehapt/ mag kein Christ vernainen/ der nur zwo ungleiche naturen da ahn ihm wil bekhennen/" As to the glorified Christ, however, Schw. held virtually a monothelitic position, as we shall see.

[2] VII, 661 f. "...gott in Christo nicht etwas one seinen menschen thut/ redt oder wirckt/ widerumb der mensch in Christo nichts one Gott leidet/ ysset/ schlafft/ sonst wurde die dispensation unnd Ernidrigung nicht auff den gantzen Christum gelangen." The similarity to the orthodox *genus apotelesmaticum* of the *communicatio idiomatum* is apparent. Cf. also VII, 613, 617, 619.

Now [in the state of glorification] the human nature of Christ is the same as the divine in might, power, and honor, just as formerly in the personal dispensation the divine nature was, for a time, united in the flesh to the human in shame, weakness, and dishonor... and was made equal in servitude, Phil. 2. (III, 249).

Significantly, also, Schwenckfeld referred such Scriptural texts as John 14 : 28 – "The Father is greater than I" – Matthew 20 : 23, Mark 13 : 32, John 6 : 38, and Hebrews 5 : 7 not only to Christ's human nature as such, but, in the interests of unity, to the entire person of Jesus in the state of humiliation, including the divine nature (VII, 635, 655-57).

In most other passages, however, Schwenckfeld maintained that the divine nature was neither weakened, lessened, nor changed in the humiliation. Not circumscribed by the flesh, the Word was also in heaven with the Father as Jesus walked on earth and ruled the world while he was dying on the cross (VII, 671). During the earthly ministry of Christ, the divine nature experienced a humiliation and a divestiture, not a cancellation, extinction, emptying, conversion, or transformation of the *forma Dei*.[1] Schwenckfeld's explanation of the kenosis rather approximates the seventeenth-century kenosis χρήσεως of Giessen: although Christ was never without the divine nature in the humiliation, he did not at all times fully make use of it before his glorification.[2] In this manner Schwenckfeld tried to avoid such a fusion or total unification in Christ as would suspend the separation of natures, or sacrifice divinity in the state of humiliation and humanity in the state of exaltation. We may add in advance that Schwenckfeld had greater success withstanding the former than the latter sacrifice.

One significant component of Schwenckfeld's doctrine of the person of Christ in humiliation remains to be discussed in prelude to his teaching concerning the glorified Lord. As a corollary to his stress on the unity of Jesus' person, his non-creaturity, and the ultimate glorification of his flesh, Schwenckfeld propounded a gradual or progressive deification (*Gottwerdung*) of Christ's humanity which originated already in the state of humiliation. He never provided a systematic explanation of this process, but based his principle on

---

[1] IX, 316, 785. Dorner, *op. cit.*, p. 635, is therefore correct in concluding: "...jene Entausserung (Nichtgebrauch seiner Majestat) bezieht sich also blos auf sein Sein in Jesu." Cf. also Herman Schultz, *Die Lehre von der Gottheit Christi* (Gotha, 1881), p. 280. "Zwar hat Schwenkfeld von einer wirklichen Kenosis des Logos nichts gelehrt."

[2] VII, 329. Cf., however, VII, 680 ff., where Schw. states that Christ *hid* his divinity during the office of our redemption, thus implying the kenosis χρύψις of Tubingen. Here Schw. is following Cyril, cf. *Opera* (Basel, 1566), IV, 132 ff.

Luke 2 : 52, emphasizing that the child Jesus "grew in wisdom and favor *before God....*" From the moment of incarnation on, the humanity of Christ grew progressively in divinity until it achieved complete equality with God.[1] In this growth the two natures of Jesus underwent a process approaching equalization, the human nature, in its susceptibility to deity, being constantly improved, penetrated, and perfected by the divine nature, which itself required no growth of this kind since the Word was no more or no less than God.[2] This deification began first in the soul of Christ and, shortly thereafter, proceeded to his body as well. Total deification, however, was not realized before the state of exaltation, when all inequalities between the human and the divine natures in Christ were surmounted.[3] Schwenckfeld admitted that previously he had regarded the glorification of Jesus as possible only after his earthly nature had been abandoned through suffering and death. Later, however, he held that the divine nature had progressively enriched the flesh, for which reason the transfiguration, for example, took place shortly before the crucifixion (VII, 339). He volunteered no further details on this doctrine because he considered it a "great mystery," in view of which one should rather concern himself with the Lord's total glorification (XII, 411).

b. *The Work of Christ*

Through his reading of Cyril and the Greek fathers, Schwenckfeld became the chief exponent of eastern physical soteriology in the Reformation Era. According to his system, salvation is rooted in the humanity of Christ, what happens to that humanity, and what happens

---

[1] IX, 787· "Das ist/ dass sich die Gottheit/ gnade und gottliche weissheit/ welche gantz volkommen in Christo dem Worte war/ auch ins Fleisch Christi algemach/ja immer je mehr habe ergossen/ es habe das Fleisch darinnen gewachsen und zugenommen/ die himlische Sonne hat jren gantzen glantz nicht auff ein mahl am Menschen Christo lassen erscheinen/... Sie gehet aller erst und langsam in der zeit zum gewechse Christi auff/ Nach dem sich der Geist jmmer stercker unnd krefftiger mit seinem göttlichen Reichthumb am Menschen Christo erzeigt und beweiset/ biss so lang das Fleisch und Blut Christi zu der Klarheit Gottes gantz volkommen worden/ und die verheissunge des heiligen Geists vom Vater/ Act. 2. Ja das gantze göttliche wesen inn aller fulle Gottes hat erreicht und eingenommen/ Denn Christus muste zuuor sterben und leiden/ unnd also in seine Gloria durch Creutz und leiden eingehen." Cf. also VI, 425; VII, 734-37.

[2] III, 464; VII, 333, 721; IX, 316.

[3] IX, 690. Some vacillation, however, can be observed of Schw. in regard to this theologoumenon, cf., e.g., IX, 710· "[Das Empfangnis]... auch ein anfang der Gottwerdung mocht genand werden/ wiewol ich... dz Vocabel Gottwerdunge des Menschens in Christo/ lieber nach dem Consumatum est, will brauchen/ und auff die Glorificationem Christi referiren/ Auch umb des Spruchs willen/ Joh. · 7. Spiritus nondum erat, Quia Iesus nondum erat glorificatus."

to the Christian through the apprehension and appropriation of that humanity. "There is no other way into the kingdom of God than through the humanity – the body, flesh, and blood – of Christ." [1] To the extent that the flesh of Jesus became progressively glorified, deified, and active in man's behalf, to that degree did it possess soteriological significance for mankind (IX, 768). Thus Schwenckfeld posited a progression in the value for the believer of Christ's person and work which paralleled his gradual glorification: "The flesh of Christ was useful from birth on and became more useful on the cross since he redeemed us therein. But to become life-giving it had first through glorification to be made useful for us (IX, 768).

The soteriological significance of the Incarnation in Schwenckfeldian theology derives from the fact that with the Word's assuming flesh, God's plan of salvation for mankind – that a sinless, non-creaturely flesh should redeem a sinful, creaturely flesh and enable its participation in the divine nature – was initiated. In fact, Schwenckfeld's entire system is an extended commentary on the phrase, "God became man in order that man might become God or what God is." [2] In the fullness of time, the Son of God assumed sinless human flesh, improved and glorified it through divine power, and conducted it to heaven in order that he might draw after him all other believing flesh.[3] The entire process of salvation had first to take place in the humanity of Christ and become authored and prefigured in his person before that humanity, in turn, could impart grace and salvation to other flesh (VII, 777 f.). By itself, therefore, the Incarnation had no conclusive significance. It rather marked the beginning of a process which found its completion only in the state of exaltation.

With a soteriology patterned after the Greek substantial theory of the redemption, we might expect that the vicarious suffering and death of Christ would be less emphasized in Schwenckfeldian theology. Such, in fact, is the case. Teaching an Alexandrian Christology and a realistic soteriology, the Silesian reformer is more a son of the East than the West. In his theology, the cross does not have that centrality

---

[1] X, 437. Cf. also VII, 792· "Das das flaisch unnd blut Christi/ nicht allein ein flaisch und blut Gottes sei/ sonder das der geist gottes auch von disem fleische unnd blute in alle wargleubige hertzen abgehe/ und das kein ander weg in himmel/ weder durch diss flaisch und blut sei." Cf· also the influence of Tauler on Schw.'s concept of the soteriological significance of Christ's deified humanity, *Sermones des hochgeleerten... doctoris Johannis Thauleri* (Augsburg, 1508), p. Ccvii], and X, 437.

[2] VI, 81; cf. also VII, 320, 593, 605. The influence of Cyril and Hilary upon this dictum is especially evident.

[3] III, 387, cf. John 12 : 32.

in God's plan of salvation attributed to it by the other reformers, particularly Luther. Schwenckfeld, however, was far from dismissing such doctrines as the historical redemption and the vicarious atonement. He regarded as the climax of the state of humiliation Jesus' accomplishment (*Leistung*) for man, i.e., his substitutionary suffering and death on the cross by which the atonement, reconciliation, and redemption were effected. Schwenckfeld protested against any disparagement of Christ's passion and death, or any questioning of their historical reality as the single, objective atonement for sin. Indeed, he even stated that almost the entire basis of salvation rested upon this article. [1] In discussing the doctrine of the atonement, Schwenckfeld, with most of the reformers, expressed himself both in Anselmic terms as well as Ransom-theory phraseology.[2] The historical redemption [3] he interpreted as the process, effected through Jesus' sacrificial death and victory over Satan, by which mankind was delivered from sin, death, hell, and the power of the Devil.[4] Christ storming the gates of hell and triumphing over Satan as the personal payment (*weergelt*) and redemption of mankind is a typical Schwenckfeldian portrayal of the mode of Jesus' saving "accomplishment." [5]

[1] IV, 521 ff. Other passages in which a typical western soteriology is expressed include. II, 555; IV, 553, 687 ff.; VII, 821. Daniel Schenkel, *Das Wesen des Protestantismus aus den Quellen des Reformationszeitalters dargestellt* (Schaffhausen, 1862), pp. 385 f., exaggerates Schw.'s lesser concern with the atonement "Er fragt nicht ohne Spott, wie der Glaube an den suhnenden Tod Christi die Sunden wegzunehmen vermoge." So also Hodge, *op. cit*, I, 83· "With him, as with Mystics generally, the ideas of guilt and expiation were ignored." *Per contra* – Dorner, *Geschichte, etc.*, p. 178, is closer to the truth "Ebenso will er zwar Christi Leiden ganz und gar mit der Kirche seine versohnende Bedeutung lassen; aber erinnert, dass man nicht scheiden durfe zwischen Christi Person und Verdienst." Even if the doctrine of the atonement is ultimately peripheral to the core of Schw.'s physical soteriology, the vicarious suffering and death of Christ are Biblical concepts, and, as a Biblicist, Schw. had to accord them something more than nominal recognition in his system.

[2] IV, 426, 521; VII, 679 ff.; IX, 296.

[3] Schw. distinguished between a *historical* redemption, accomplished by Jesus in the state of humiliation (redemption in the orthodox and underived sense); and an *applied* redemption, communicated to the believer by the glorified Christ in the state of exaltation (XII, 963; XV, 3).

[4] II, 555; IV, 687 ff.; VI, 630, IX, 296 ff.; XII, 963.

[5] IV, 552, 687 ff., 690; VI, 625-27; VII, 636 ff. The terms "bezalung," "weergelt", and "erlosunge" occur frequently as designations of Christ in his redemptive function during the state of humiliation.

Many passages in Schw. also indicate the living function of the cross in the life of the believer, i.e., his imitation of Christ in patiently enduring whatever suffering is sent by God, subduing the flesh, and the like. Schw. himself brought out an edition of Thomas à Kempis' (?) *Imitatio Christi ca.* 1531, IV, Doc. CXXIII, and the cross is, in fact, frequently interpreted by Schw. in an ethical sense, cf. IV, 704; V, 738; IX, 471; and XI, 892. Maron, *op. cit.*, p. 42, however, stresses the ethical significance too highly when he terms it "Letzte Bedeutung des Kreuzes…

Besides satisfaction, atonement, and redemption, the cross had also another meaning for Schwenckfeld which better answered the needs of his physical soteriological system. What happened to the body of Jesus in its crucifixion and death he regarded as crucially important in God's plan of salvation. For, despite his positing a gradual deification of Christ's flesh during the humiliation, the passion of Jesus represented for Schwenckfeld an abrupt disjuncture between the states of humiliation and exaltation. It involved a putting to death of the old humanity, a purging of its weaknesses and earthly limitations, a necessary sloughing off of the former existence so that the new being of Christ's glorified flesh could arise from the ashes of the old and exist in its ultimate and most useful soteriological state, i.e., where it was of a consistency and in a posture to communicate itself to the believer (VII, 340, 571). In this connection Schwenckfeld was fond of citing John 12 : 24: "...unless a grain of wheat falls into the earth and dies, it remains alone; but if it dies, it bears much fruit."

In Schwenckfeldian theology, therefore, the atonement, satisfaction, and redemption — the whole state of humiliation, in fact — had the same necessarily unfinished character as the Incarnation so far as man's salvation was concerned. For humanity had still to be saved from sin and creaturity, and although the flesh of the Savior had transcended this ruin and this separation from the divine nature, it had not yet assumed that glorified, spiritual form by which it could communicate itself to all of believing humanity so as to free it from sin and creaturity as well. Therefore the glorification of Christ's humanity and his true apprehension in the present state of exaltation rather than in his humiliation became for Schwenckfeld a simple soteriological necessity:

> For although the flesh and blood of Christ [were] in themselves clean, holy, righteous, etc. in his nature from the beginning, how would they help or prove useful to me? For they could not come into my heart, nor could the blood of Christ besprinkle me to heal and rectify the injuries of my soul. Therefore they had first to become a vitalizing, sanctifying flesh and blood — yes, spirit and life in Christ — and to assume the essence of God. Then can I, poor sinner, benefit from them as they are today, praise God (XII, 654)

For this reason, Schwenckfeld never tired of contrasting the states of humiliation and exaltation both from a christological and soteriological point of view. The dichotomy which he had avoided in the

---

fur Schw." His understanding of the cross is really mediating: it constitutes both expiation and example for the believer, gift and responsibility, IV, 227. Cf. also IX, 500; XII, 769.

person of Jesus found massive expression in his distinction between the two states – Schwenckfeld really used the term "beings," "existences" (*Wesen*) – of Christ's person.¹ The believer's *Erkenntnis Christi* was thereby bifurcated because of its double object. Knowing Jesus in humiliation as the crucified Lord was to partake of "the milk-teaching in Christ," said Schwenckfeld; but understanding him in glory was "the strong, bold food." ² And any discerning Christian, not to say theologian, should definitely come beyond the "milk" stage.³ His criticism of Article III: *De Filio Dei* in the *Confessio Augustana* is illuminating in this regard:

> In this article, however, one must further consider... that the Lord Jesus Christ wishes to be known and believed by us not only according to the flesh and in a historical manner, that is, not only with reason, or according to... how he was born, died, taught and lived, what he suffered for us, what he earned and accomplished for us through his suffering; but he wishes much rather to be understood and pondered after the spirit and his new, glorified, entirely heavenly being, as a reigning Lord and king of heaven and earth... and as a donor and administrator of all heavenly properties... Therefore also Paul says: Even though we once knew Christ after the flesh, we know him thus no longer. II Cor. 5 (III, 888)

In summary, the work of Jesus in the state of humiliation consisted in atoning for sin by his suffering and dying, redeeming man from death and the power of Satan, and gaining, in his flesh, those divine qualities and benefits which he would later distribute through that flesh in the state of glorification (VII, 831). The humanity of Christ, however, was not yet in a posture to mediate itself together with its qualities and benefits in order to apply to the believer his objective salvation from sin and creaturity. That earthly humanity, therefore, was purged by suffering and death that it might be glorified and deified.

---

[1] III, 266, *et passim*. Hence Luther's accusation that Schw. was really making "einen doppelten Christus" by his sharp contrast of the person and work of Christ in the states of humiliation and exaltation, cf. *Luthers Sämmtliche Wercke* (Erlangen, 1830 ff.), LVIII, 29 ff.

Schoeps, *op. cit.*, p. 35, is mistaken in interpreting the two states of Christ as "...zweier verschiedener Zustande in der irdischen Existenzweise Christi," one earthly, mortal from an Adamite nature; and the other susceptible to gradual deification. The "Zweier Stande" refer rather to the states of humiliation and exaltation.

[2] "die milchlehre inn Christo," and "die starcke kecke speise," after Heb. 5 . 12; cf. IX, 147-49, *et passim*. Schw. maintained that even during his earthly ministry Jesus was interpreted spiritually by the believer, who saw his second state by faith even during the first through divine revelation! Cf. VII, 347, 354 f.

[3] Later in life, Schw. acknowledged that many found his teachings concerning the glory of Christ "too high and too hard" to understand. Tolerantly he prescribed the "milk diet" for the weaker, cf. IX, 500.

CHAPTER X

CHRIST IN THE STATE OF EXALTATION

(3. *Die Glorificierung Christi*)

a. The Person of Christ

"He descended into hell; the third day He rose again from the dead; He ascended into heaven and sitteth on the right hand of God the Father Almighty; from thence He shall come to judge the quick and the dead." Here, as in its other clauses, Schwenckfeld accepted the wording of *The Creed* unqualifiedly (VII, 519, *et passim*).

The *descensus ad inferos*, as has been observed, pertained only to the Word and the soul of Christ's humanity. Since, however, the soul is *potissima humanitatis pars*, the descent into hell with its triumph over Satan could be interpreted as the first stage of the full glorification of Jesus' humanity, although Schwenckfeld never stated this explicitly. Hell he regarded as a spatiotemporal reality, a locality for punishing the damned. He strictly opposed any attenuation of the term as signifying merely despair or death.[1] We have already noted how Christ triumphed over Satan and released the souls of the believing fathers from limbo, thus fulfilling his initial function as glorified Redeemer.[2]

Schwenckfeld regarded the resurrection as "...an ineffable high rebirth of Christ's flesh from and in God.... The birth from the dead brought and gave to the man in Christ to possess naturally what the Word from eternity had, was, and possessed naturally from God the Father.[3] Also according to his humanity was Jesus now "equal and consubstantial to God."[4] The process of the progressive deification of Christ's flesh, begun at the Incarnation but terminated temporarily

---

[1] X, 360 ff.; cf. also Crautwald's definition in VI, 146.

[2] Cf. *supra*, pp. 51 and 68.

[3] VII, 740. For a concise summary of Christ's glorification, see "Von der Aufferstehung/ Erscheinung unnd verclerunge Christi" (after 1541?) to be published as Doc. MCCXIX in XVII.

[4] *Ibid.*: "eines Wesens unnd gleicher Gott."

by a quasi-purgative passion and death, now virtually attained its object: full glorification, deification, and equality with God.

And yet the process was not quite complete. Rather, Schwenckfeld noted a progressive deification of Jesus' humanity also in the initial stages of the exaltation. There was, for example, the problem of the resurrected body of Christ which seemed, as yet, amenable to human circumscriptions during the forty days of his post-resurrection appearances. Schwenckfeld interpreted the manifestations in which Jesus ate with his disciples and was touched by them not only as gracious dispensations to inculcate faith in the resurrection, but also as indications that Christ was still "to some extent" on earth.[1] He had not yet ascended to his Father, nor received that plentitude of glory which he would assume in the session at the right hand of God.[2] Therefore the asseveration in Matthew 28 : 18, "All authority in heaven and in earth has been given me," was interpreted by Schwenckfeld as a prelude to that total assumption of divine power and glory by Jesus which followed his ascension and session (VI, 484).

The consummation of Christ's glorification, then, took place with his session at the right hand of the Father. Not in thirty years of theologizing did Schwenckfeld ever define the right hand of God as a locally circumscribed place.[3] On the other hand, he did not subscribe to Luther's definition of the right hand as "everywhere" in the interests of supporting a ubiquity of Christ's body.[4] His own interpretation was not always uniform. Sometimes he defined the right hand as Christ himself (III, 208), or the Word as Hand of God through which all things were created (III, 213, 242). Elsewhere it is God himself (III, 220, 260). At any rate, the session at the right hand of the Father constituted the final stage of the glorification of Christ – the full deification of his humanity:

[1] Schw., however, took care not to stress the physical aspects of such theophanies. The Christ who could be touched by his disciples was also the Lord who passed through closed doors (XI, 578). Cf. also VI, 483 ff.; XI, 530.

[2] VII, 773. In another passage, however, Schw. implies that total deification took place at the moment of resurrection – VII, 558: "[Christ arose]... durch die Allmachtige Gottliche krafft... mit welcher er auch nach dem flaische jnn der wunderbarlichen widergeburt von den todten/ augenplicklich gantz ist vergottet /gesalbet und durchgossen/"

[3] Cf., e.g., VII, 786 "...sollich Sitzen/ stett/ ortt oder stul (wie die schrifft dauon redt) keiner umbschreibung/ keines leiblichen zirckels/ raums/ noch Creaturlicher abmessung bedurffe/ sonder der himmel selbst/ die ewige wonunge gottes/ das uberhimlische wesen und seine almechtige Maiesteet sei."

[4] III, 208; cf. *WA*, XXIII, 142.

"Christ sits at the right hand of God" is the same as saying that the human nature of Christ is equal to the divine in might and honor; for Christ, true God and man, is now entirely indivisible and wholly named from each nature. It is as much as saying that the body and blood of Christ are in the eternal, living Word; that the flesh has the power, honor, glory, and perfection which the Word and Son of God possessed from the Father before this world existed .. [1]

Let us now finally examine what Schwenckfeld meant by the glorification (*Verklarung, Glorificierung*) and deification (*Vergottung, Gottwerdung*) [2] of Christ's flesh or humanity. Glorification signified that the body of Jesus was transfigured and clothed with nothing less than the eminence, glory, and radiance of God. And since, to Schwenckfeld's mind, divine glory was nothing less than the very essence of God, glorification and deification are used synonymously in his writings (VI, 484; VII, 516). Deification he qualified as follows:

> We define the deification of Christ not as an augmentation of his divine nature, nor a diminution of his human nature, but rather as an equalization of the man, Christ, with God: the glorification of the flesh in unity... with the Word through the anointing of God, and its exaltation to and in the right hand of God.[3]

Schwenckfeld often used verbal clusters in delineating the process of glorification. Thus the flesh of Christ was "improved, renewed, glorified and deified" (VII, 338); "thoroughly anointed, deified, fired, entirely saturated with the divine essence" (VII, 345); "bodily filled with the eternal deity, fired, and completely... deified" (VII, 516); "united [with the divine nature], changed, altered, improved," and deprived of all such creaturely *idiomata* as eating, sleeping, and the like (VII, 564). In fine, the humanity of Christ in glory had completely abandoned its earthly *Wesen* and assumed the heavenly (III, 202).[4]

---

[1] III, 212; cf. also VII, 785; VIII, 393.

[2] Although technically these terms imply a distinction as between θεοποιέω and ἀποθεόω, Schw. uses *Vergottung* and *Gottwerdung* interchangeably, cf., e.g., VIII, 667.

[3] VIII, 667; cf. also VIII, 722. For the Biblical citations which Schw. lists in support of this doctrine, see VIII, 666 ff. Cyril, *Opera* (Basel, 1566), I, 19, is cited by Schw., VII, 758 ff., as supporting a deification of the human nature of Christ in glory; so also Hilary, VII, 592 ff., cf. *MSL*, 10· 33, 85, 283, *et passim*. Similarly, Schw. often quotes Ambrose on the glorification of Christ, VII, 741; cf. *MSL*, 16, 1341. Cf. esp VII, 752 ff., where Schw. lists other parallels between Ambrosian doctrine and his own. Irenaeus is cited by Schw. not only for his recapitulation theory of the atonement, but also for his views on the glorification of Christ, VII, 756-58; cf. *Opera* (Leipzig, 1853), 524 ff. For a general list of Schw.'s patristic citations, see XI, 136.

[4] Ecke, *op. cit.*, pp. 124 f., restricts the implications of *Vergottung* beyond the intentions of Schw. "Dieses Verklaren nennt Schwenckfeld ofters 'Vergotten,' ein Ausdruck, der nach seiner ausdrucklichen Versicherung mit naturhafter Gottwerdung nichts zu tun hat, sondern

The Schwenckfeldian doctrine of the consummate glorification-deification of Christ's flesh raises the problem as to what remains of the *man* who has become God. In the state of exaltation it is not the divine, but the human nature which gives intellectual pause. Let us examine first the divine attributes which Schwenckfeld ascribes to the humanity of the glorified Lord, then the human properties which remain, and, finally, the relationship between the divine and the human natures in the state of exaltation.

Schwenckfeld's most consistent definition of the deification of Jesus' humanity is equalization (*Gleichwerdung*), i.e., that the divine and human natures now have a fundamental equality in essence, character, attributes, properties, powers, and office.[1] The humanity of Christ has received divine honor and glory and become the object of adoration and prayer not only by reason of the *unio personalis* and a *communicatio idiomatum*, but because the human nature itself now possesses the divine *idiomata* as its own. Any *communicatio*, therefore, is especially unnecessary in the state of glory (VII, 489); or rather, a *communicatio* is, indeed, pertinent, but a *"communicatio idiomatum naturalis, vera, propria"* because both natures are now equal (VII, 714). Jesus is Lord and God not only according to the one nature, but also according to the other (IV, 19; VII, 518, *et passim*). "There is nothing in Christ today which is not God or that which God is. Otherwise one would expel the man Jesus Christ from the one, simple essence of the Holy Trinity" (IV, 30). Schwenckfeld could accord the humanity of Christ no greater honor: *it had become part of the Trinity itself!*[2]

Complementing this stress on the present divine aspects of Christ's humanity is a parallel rejection of all human *accidentia* and properties which would circumscribe or restrict his glorified flesh. Obviously the principal *accidens* which Schwenckfeld jettisoned was creaturity, which, to be sure, he had rejected as an attribute of Jesus already in

---

lediglich das biblische δοξάζειν auf Grund von 2. Petr. 1, 4 veranschaulichen will als ein 'ganz herrliches, gottliches, geistliches Durchsalben und Verklaren.' " By *Vergottung* Schw. intended not just transfiguration or glorification, but the ultimate stage of that glorification· total equality with God.

[1] VII, 338 "Er [Christus] hat aber nu kein ander wesen/ denn das wesen Gottes." Cf. also VII, 564, where Schw. states that the heavenly man has become everything essentially which God is. All divine *idiomata* and attributes are in his possession.

[2] IV, 30, VI, 82, VII, 571. In VII, 573 f., Schw. cites Augustine, *de bono perseverantiae*, MSL, 45, 1033; 192, 773, as testifying that the Word and glorified flesh constitute the Second Person of the Trinity; Alcuin is also quoted in this connection, cf. VIII, 344, and MSL 101, 43 ff.

the state of humiliation. He had done so, however, primarily as a preparatory safeguard that absolutely no suggestion of creatureliness should accompany Christ into the glorified state. Schwenckfeld's original aversion to the term "creature" in Christology, we will remember, pertained only to the glorified Lord.[1] But now any creaturely *idiomata* whatsoever, especially servitude, materiality, visibility, biological restrictions, mortality, and the like would have excluded the humanity of Christ from the essence of the Trinity, which could not tolerate in itself such contrarieties to divinity.[2] Similarly, all such temporal and spatial circumscriptions of Jesus' humanity as finitude, dimension, and proportion were also abandoned with the death of Christ (VII, 338, 502). With Luther, Schwenckfeld was especially infuriated at what he regarded the Swiss concept of Christ's local presence in glory: his sitting in some celestial corner, so to speak. He was particularly nettled by a diagram of the Trinity drawn by Bullinger in which the humanity of the glorified Lord was circled out of the Godhead:

> Whoever says that Jesus the man is now outside the divine essence in a corporeal place and is circumscribed with the dimensions of a creature not only places an imperfection and inequality in the unity of the Holy Trinity, but also divides the one, glorious person of Christ, places the humanity under the divinity, knows Christ after the flesh, and does not let him be equal to God *per omnia*. He does not glorify Christ, for to be locally present pertains to an imperfect being It belongs far under God, since the place is always broader and larger than what is circumscribed and comprehended therein (VI, 82).

Thus far Schwenckfeld's doctrine bears close resemblance to a modified Eutychianism which introduces the monophysitism with the state of exaltation rather than the Incarnation. What, if anything, remains of the *human* qualities of the human nature in Schwenckfeld's concept of the glorified Christ? Here, obviously, is the weakest point in his entire christological structure. Well aware of his vulnerability, Schwenckfeld nevertheless strenuously insisted that he maintained intact the integrity of Christ's true humanity in glory! In fact,

---

[1] In this regard it is interesting to note how Schw.'s concern for the non-creaturity of Christ proceeds from a general recognition of his creaturity, to a denial that Jesus remained a creature in glory although the term did apply in the state of humiliation; to a negation of the possibility that Christ was a creature in either state; to a subsequent mellowing which, while continuing to deny that Christ was a creature in glory, nevertheless did *permit* (but not propose) the epithet "new creature" as a designation for Jesus in the state of humiliation, cf. IX, 111; XI, 743; XII, 614.

[2] VII, 338, 719. In VII, 571, Schw. held that the flesh of Christ was not part of the Trinity in the state of humiliation.

nothing galled him more than the charge that he denied the humanity of Jesus by equating it with divinity. He countered by asserting that Christ was still true man despite his glorification, and, so far as its continuity was concerned, with the same flesh in which he walked about on earth.[1] "Indeed, he is a true man who, also after his deification, retains – entirely unmutilated – flesh and blood, members, body, soul, mouth, eyes, and all his limbs." [2] The human nature was not "emptied, consumed, or extinguished" because of its glorification, for if the humanity of Christ were denied, he could no longer have a glorified *body* (VII, 515). In an emphatic moment Schwenckfeld even declared:

> We deny nothing in Christ, not even the smallest member in his *solido corpore*; even as in his ascension he left behind him neither flesh nor blood, yes, not a little hair, so to speak, which belonged to the perfection of his human nature, but led his entire humanity upward into the glory and essence of God his father (VII, 776).

What kind of humanity this might be is described, with Schwenckfeld's editorial approval, by Valentine Crautwald:

> Christ, to be sure, has a face as well as limbs and is a perfect man But such a man as no painter can paint, nor carver carve, nor founder cast. The countenance of Christ is God his father . . The nose of this face breathes divine essence from itself; and the mouth of this man speaks the sentence and judgement of God. The eyes shine with earnest over the godless and with tenderness over the godly (VI, 245).

The glorification of Jesus' flesh, therefore, involved its spiritualization, but a spiritualization which did not deny the reality of that flesh (VIII, 644 f.).

If Schwenckfeld was seriously literal regarding his doctrine of the deification of Christ's humanity – and he was – then the human properties and attributes which are said to remain in the state of glory would seem nothing more than mere tropes. In fact, that a human nature should remain at all in the exaltation would seem little more than a concession to Chalcedonian orthodoxy, necessary if Schwenckfeld were not to go the way of Eutyches. But the reformer would hasten to object. In his reasoning he posited a double epistemology. There are two kinds of truth: one earthly, human, and

---

[1] IV, 793. H. Schultz, *op. cit.*, pp. 280 f., denies any continuity between the earthly "created" (*sic*) flesh of Christ and his heavenly humanity in Schw.'s Christology.

[2] VII, 337. Cf. XIV, 403 f "...die/ welche Christum nu nach dem einnemen seiner Gottlichen herrlicheit und klarheit mit wolten einen waren menschen von leib/ seel/ blut unnd fleisch sein oder bleiben lassen/ oder aber ihnen seiner menschlichen Gleidmass einigerley weise berauben/ aussleren und bestummeln wolten/ mit denen ichs kurtzumb nicht halte." Cf. also VII, 515.

creaturely; the other heavenly, divine, and spiritual. The former is apprehended by natural, unenlightened reason; the latter, by faith (VII, 599 ff.). While reason and natural truth would be compelled to deny the reality of Jesus' humanity in glory, Christ does remain a true man despite his exaltation according to divine truth and faith (VII, 760). Not *physice* but *theologice* does Christ have a genuine *solidum corpus* with all its members in glory (VII, 767).

In defending himself against the charge of compromising the humanity of Jesus in the state of exaltation, Schwenckfeld also advanced another argument which stemmed from his soteriology. Far from surrendering his humanity, the glorified Christ had attained the very highest development which God had intended for man. He was now the true, ideal human being, i.e., one who was sinless, non-creaturely, and participating fully in the divine nature. And sharing in the essence of God, instead of contradicting the idea of humanity, rather fulfilled the original aim of man's creation (IX, 983; XV, 170). Thus the Second Adam was actually the first true man, as compared with the first Adam who was only a figurative man before God.[1]

Moreover, so far as denying the humanity of Jesus was concerned, Schwenckfeld asserted that not honoring, rather than honoring, the flesh of Christ was equivalent to denying it.

> Those much rather deny or despise the humanity of Christ in exaltation who deprive the man Jesus Christ of his divine honor and glory; who wish to circle him out of the essence of the Holy Trinity; who also do not let his body, flesh, and blood remain the true food and drink of the soul – rather than Caspar Schwenckfeld, who gives the Lord Christ his divine honor and believes and confesses him also according to his humanity as Lord of all things (XII, 56).

It is a fact that the Christology of Schwenckfeld is devoted predominantly to the human, not the divine, nature of Jesus. And what he predicated of Christ's exalted humanity was not, he maintained, intended to compromise it but to glorify it. Schwenckfeld's ultimate argument, therefore, was that augmentation could not mean extinction.

The relationship between the divine and human natures in the state of glorification is characterized by a unity even more complete, if possible, than in the state of humiliation. For now no progressive deification of Jesus' flesh was necessary; no non-divine properties existed which required purging from his humanity. The Word and the

---

[1] XV, 170: "Adam war am erst ein bildlicher mensch vor Gott/ er war noch nicht ein mensch/ sondern nur ein bildt des waren menschens/ Christi/ darnach wird die warheit dem bildt eingeschrieben/ Daher kompt der new mensch." Cf. also XIII, 572.

flesh were now fully equal in essence, property, function, and office. Why, then, not a single nature in the exalted Lord, a complete fusion of the human and the divine? Because from such a mixture, Schwenckfeld protested, either a *tertium quid* would result, or divinity would absorb humanity, which would be intolerable.[1]

But of monophysitism, Eutychianism, mixture or fusion of the natures, transformation of the one nature into the other, or the absorption of humanity into divinity Schwenckfeld was accused, as previously observed. We have noted how he answered such charges against his Christology of the state of humiliation. Could he, however, justifiably escape these censures against his doctrine of the deified humanity of Christ, which predicated a personal unity even more intimate than in the state of humiliation? Once again, in his Ephesian interpretation of Chalcedonian orthodoxy, Schwenckfeld strove to maintain the integrity of the two natures in the one glorified Lord. With repeated emphasis he insisted that deification did not involve a transformation, transfiguration, conversion, or metamorphosis (*Verwandlung*)[2] of the human nature into the divine, or a fusion of the two natures (VII, 455 ff., 724):

> However that they [theologians at Schmalkalden, 1540] write· "Schwenckfeld holds or intends that the human nature is transformed into the divine" is absolutely untrue Christ still possesses both natures entirely and completely. His human nature, however, has been received into God[3] and participates in all divine honor, power, and might from the

[1] XIV, 680 f. In a rare passage, however, Schw. did admit the possibility of the term "mixture" as characterizing the union of Christ's natures, but he carefully guarded his statement: "Die allten lerer/ nicht Ireneus allein (dauon Vadianus schreibt) sonder Terullianus [sic] Naziansenus/ ja auch Augustinus/ haben gedachte verainigung umb der onzertrenlicheit und onmuglichen sonderung willen/ aine vermischung genennet/ welches bei guttem verstande/ so ferr man nur baide naturen darbei gantz behelt/ und nicht ain gedrits auff Christo macht wol steen kond/ und wer sonderlich der tailer halben diser zeit von noten zubedencken," VII, 628. Cf. also XII, 526, where Schw. cited Melanchthon on the use of "mixture." Schw., however, maintained· "...solcher rede von der Mixtur nie habe [ich] gebrauchet."

[2] Schw. uses the terms "wandeln," "andern," "bessern," "erneuern," "verklaren," "vergotten," instead of "umwandeln" or "verwandeln." The following is Schw.'s definition of "verwandeln," VII, 717 f.. "Denn daas haissen wir hie verwandelt/ wenn ain ding inns ander auffhorlich wirt verkheeret/ oder dadurch verzeret/ verschluckt/ Absorbiret/ Also das es nach seiner natur abgetilgkt und nicht mer da ist/.... Nu ist aber die menschait Christi/ durch die verklerung nicht inn die Gotthait verwandelt/ Es ist der mensch inn Christo nicht also verwandelt/ das er durch sein gotwerdung abgetilcket und nimer sei/ ja so wenig Gott in der menschwerdung Gott zusein hat auffgehoret/ so wenig hat der mensch im wesen gottes/ mit Gott vereiniget unnd vergottet/ ain mensch zusein auffgehoret." In 1528, however, Schw. had stated that the earthly "wesen" of Christ had been "verwandelt" into the heavenly, II, 202.

[3] "inn Gott auffgenommen." Here Schw. draws a hairbreadth distinction, cf. VII, 718: "Die menscheit ist nit zur gothait worden/ sonder der mensche ist Gott worden."

nature of the Word. In the glorification of Christ no transformation of one nature into the other has taken place, but an equalization of both natures in glory.[1]

Schwenckfeld's favorite explanation as to how a glorification-deification of Christ's flesh could take place without hopelessly compromising its true humanity was the converse analogy of the Incarnation. As fundamental to his soteriology, we will remember, Schwenckfeld postulated a divine-human reciprocation in the person of Christ: "God became man in order that man might become what God is" (VI, 81). But this reciprocity was not effected through a direct transformation of God to man, and then man, in turn, to God:

> Even as, by divine design, the Word was made flesh, so now after the complete dispensation, the flesh, in turn, was made Word, in both cases the distinction between the natures in the unity of the person having been maintained. For even as the Word of God was neither extinguished nor changed in the first *cursus*, nor ceased to be the Word of the great God however much it was united with the flesh in ignominy and affliction; so in the second *cursus*, in turn, the flesh is neither abolished, nor ceases to be flesh even if it has been made one with the Word and participates in all the glory and efficacy of the Word....[2]

Schwenckfeld thus interprets the glorification of Christ as a kind of incarnation in reverse, an "inverbation" or spiritualization of the flesh. But just as the Word was not transformed into the flesh in the *Menschwerdung*, so also the flesh was not converted into the Word in the *Gottwerdung*.

The closest that Schwenckfeld ever theoretically approached monophysitism was in an unconfessed monothelitism which he had denied for the state of humiliation, but virtually conceded in the exaltation. At first he held that both a divine and a human will persisted in glory, the human will, however, having been spiritualized, deified, and rendered virtually indistinguishable from the divine (VIII, 377). Although both natures possessed separate wills, these wills were identical, so that there was but "one will, one operation, and one being" in both natures (VIII, 647 f.). Ultimately and logically, however, Schwenckfeld rejected the "error... concerning two wills" and maintained that Christ had a homogeneous will in glory.[3]

The question remains as to whether Schwenckfeld retained any real distinction between the two natures of Jesus in the state of

---

[1] VII, 503; cf. also VII, 718.

[2] IV, 21. See also IV, 793; VII, 520, 592 ff., 717. Cf. the possible influence of Hilary on Schw.'s argument, VII, 592 ff., and Hilary, *MSL*, *loc. cit.*

[3] IX, 167: "...einigen willen und einerlai wesen."

exaltation, besides preserving for the flesh of Christ those glorified human attributes which have previously been cited. Since he held that the human nature was equal to the divine in essence, properties, and office, we should hardly anticipate any remaining discrimination whatever. Nevertheless, some vestigial differentiations between the two natures in glory do appear in the writings of Schwenckfeld, although very rarely, and these he would have been the last to emphasize. One such passage asserts that the exalted humanity of Christ did not extend to the person of the Father as did his divinity.[1] Again, "the flesh of the reigning Lord Christ is not the divine being, but the other nature of Christ in the divine being" (IX, 766). Elsewhere, pressed by his opponents, Schwenckfeld did acknowledge that a certain precedence was to be accorded the divine nature as source for the glory of Christ's humanity: "...the eternal, almighty Word in the personal union with the flesh is the foundation and beginning in every way and maintains the precedence. Thus all divine honor, power, might, and glory of the flesh in Christ originate from the conjoined Word."[2] Schwenckfeld immediately added, however, that since the human nature in glory was gifted by the Word with divine properties as a natural possession – not merely from a *communicatio idiomatum* – both natures of Christ were constituted and acted in equality.

A special problem in Schwenckfeld's doctrine of the glorified humanity of Christ is the question of ubiquity. Were the flesh of Jesus possessed of all the divine attributes in the state of exaltation, as Schwenckfeld maintained, would it not also be omnipresent? Although he rejected Luther's concept of the ubiquity of Christ's body as an absurdity (X, 702), the Silesian reformer was nevertheless compelled by the logic of his system to concede some kind of ubiquity to the glorified humanity of Jesus. In his early theology he had posited a

---

[1] VII, 784· "Die menschait Christi raicht nicht auff die person des vattern wie die gotthait Christi." This, however, seems inconsonant with Schw.'s assertion that the humanity of Christ had become part of the essence of the Trinity, IV, 30; VI, 82; VII, 571.

[2] VIII, 656 f. A statement, therefore, such as Maron's, *op. cit.*, p. 55, needs revision: "Schw. versucht mit seiner Lehre vom Fleisch (und Blut) Christi nichts weniger, als Wort und Geist zu eliminieren und das Amt des Wortes und des hl. Geistes dem Fleisch (und dem Blut) Christi zueignen." Even if the citation from VIII, 656 f. may be regarded as a concession to his opponents, in the bulk of other passages, Schw. stressed the *equality* of the Word and the glorified humanity of Christ in essence, attributes, and office. That the Holy Spirit is nearly equated with the glorified Lord, however, has its truth. Cf., e.g., XII, 398· "Christus ist aber heut dass/ was der heilige Geist ist." Elsewhere Schw. says that the Holy Spirit proceeds only through and on account of the flesh of Christ, V, 595; cf. also IX, 889.

sharper differentiation between the natures in the state of exaltation and held, for example, that the glorified humanity of Christ was not ubiquitous like the divine nature but limited to heaven.[1] Then, as his Christology developed, Schwenckfeld stressed the illocal presence of Jesus in glory (VI, 82, *et passim*). Next he proceeded to a virtual "selective ubiquity" which he expressed as follows: "...Christ, according to his body and blood, neither must be nor intends to be in all creatures.... When the Holy Scriptures speak of the presence, accompaniment, and attendance of Jesus Christ... they refer to him only according to that presence which he has in the believer" (III, 260).

Later in life Schwenckfeld held a broader concept of Christ's ubiquity but qualified it as a transcendental, illocal, and omniscient type of omnipresence. Because of the union and equalization of Christ's natures, where the Son of God is, there is also his glorified body; where the glorified body is, there is also the Son of God. And since divinity is omnipresent, "it must certainly follow that he [Christ] is everywhere and *ubique* also according to his body, flesh, and blood" (VII, 782). Yet *esse ubique* does not connote a local presence in all physical places, but rather a presence in the essence of God, i.e., in a being which transcends place and time, although all place and time are revealed and present to his omniscience. Schwenckfeld also continued to teach a selective ubiquity, a gracious presence of Christ in the heart of the Christian (VII, 780-84, *et passim*). Indeed, it was precisely to insure to the believer the true, efficient, saving presence of Christ's glorified body and blood that Schwenckfeld developed his Christology and dedicated his life.

To summarize, the Schwenckfeldian doctrine of the person of Christ in the state of exaltation had but two guiding concerns: 1) to stress the total unity in the person of the glorified Lord; and 2) to demonstrate that the humanity of Jesus had attained that degree of total participation in divinity that it now shared essence, attributes, and particularly all soteriological functions with the Word on the basis of full equality. Thus Schwenckfeld's Christology had been shaped by the soteriological necessity that Christ infuse his sinless, non-creaturely, glorified humanity into the heart of the Christian, that he might be delivered from sin and creaturity and enabled to participate with his Lord in the divine nature. Because of its total glorification, the humanity of Jesus was so communicable. Indeed, Word and flesh had

---

[1] III, 218-21, 260. Once, in an anonymous treatise – but without reasonable doubt from his pen – III, 528 ff , Schw. even implied that Christ's was a local presence in heaven.

become one in their soteriological functions as they were one in essence.[1]

b. *The Work of Christ*

Schwenckfeld retained orthodox terminology in describing the offices of Christ in the state of exaltation. Thus Jesus today acts as Savior, High Priest, King, Intercessor, Advocate, Future Judge, and, especially, Mediator (VII, 815-17). All of these functions, however, are to be interpreted with a double Schwenckfeldian safeguard: 1) both natures of Christ are directly, coordinately involved in all of his offices; and 2) the present activities of Jesus in glory do not connote a servitude surviving from the state of humiliation, nor an inequality in his person which would make of his humanity a servile instrument in behalf of the believer (VII, 815 ff.). This, indeed, would involve a mixing of the two states. Rather has Christ won salvation and merited all divine benefits for his followers already in the state of humiliation. His function in glory is merely the application and distribution of what he has already earned (VII, 830). The separate offices of King, High Priest, Intercessor, and the like are only variations on the central theme that Christ, as glorified Mediator between God and man, now applies to all believers that which has happened in his own person by means of his own person, i.e., through his glorified humanity as this is communicated to the Christian. In fact, Jesus' function as self-communicating, self-imparting Mediator is so existentially important to man that Schwenckfeld discusses this work of Christ in glory separately as the fourth, the most important, and the ultimate stage of the *Erkenntnis Christi*: "participation in Christ." Here, indeed, Schwenckfeldian Christology and soteriology have become identified. The division between person and work in Christ, always too artificial and systematic for the religious temper of the lay theologian, was now suspended.

[1] II, 573; VII, 345, 502, 720; VIII, 656.

CHAPTER XI

PARTICIPATION IN CHRIST – SOTERIOLOGY

(4. *Die Teilhaftigkeit Christi*)

The ultimate object of soteriology according to Schwenckfeld – man's salvation from sin and creatureliness, and the realization of his true humanity through participation in the divine nature – was achieved by means of a process which the reformer summarized "the participation in Christ," the sharing of the Christian in the glorified body of his Lord. This phenomenon, we have noted, was made possible by the fact that the humanity of Jesus after its glorification was in a posture to communicate itself to the believer in unity with the Word.[1] As a process, participation in Christ involved several component phases which Schwenckfeld designated after traditional theological terminology: redemption, satisfaction, and reconciliation, accomplished historically by Jesus in the state of humiliation; and justification, sanctification, and regeneration, which the believer appropriates spiritually from the glorified Christ in the present.[2] This terminology, however, is not to be understood as a systematic *ordo salutis*, for these functions are virtually interdependent, and the distinction between them something less than rigid in Schwenckfeld: "Therefore although the redemption, justification, reconciliation, freeing, sanctification, etc., are separate spiritual functions from the riches of the grace of God, nevertheless they are all of one essence and are to be found completely today yet in Christ, and none is to be separated from the other."[3]

[1] Cf. VII, 758, e.g., and the influence of Cyril on Schw.'s stressing the necessity of the believer's participation in the body of the glorified Lord through a spiritual communion, as well as the general soteriological efficacy of the exalted humanity of Christ, *Opera* (Basel, 1566), I, 197, 201.

[2] XII, 963-66. In relating the *ordo salutis* to the work of Christ in both states, Schw. repeatedly cited Rom. 4 : 25 as a summary of the gospel: "...Jesus our Lord... was put to death for our trespasses and raised for our justification," X, 707, *et passim*.

[3] XV, 4 f. Schw. actually preferred another way of explaining the process of participation in Christ which was not shackled by dogmatic terminology and gave freer expression to his Bible-based religiosity. VIII, 823: "Das nu widerumb Christus aber Ihm h gaiste Inn allen gleubigen muss eingeflaischt werden/ geboren/ leiden rc aufersteen/ in ainem Jeglichen nach der mass seines glaubens/ Damit er als das haupt alle glider seines leibs In sein Reich also hinach holle/" Cf. also X, 780 ff.

Schwenckfeld's understanding of the redemption, satisfaction, and reconciliation have been discussed previously. Objectively completed in themselves, these functions were nevertheless imperfect in effect until Christ's glorified state when they could be appropriated subjectively by the believer. Let us now consider the soteriological activities which Schwenckfeld assigned to the state of exaltation: justification, sanctification, and regeneration.

Again it must be emphasized that Schwenckfeld did not regard these functions as clear and distinct phases in a process of participation in Christ. They are rather reciprocal and contemporaneous divine actions, even substantial attributes of the indwelling Lord. Justification and sanctification, which the older Schwenckfeld drew ever more closely together, purge natural man from the ruin of sin, while regeneration emancipates him from the status of creaturity. All three functions prepare for – and, ultimately, effect – the believer's participation in the divine nature. Since, however, participation in Christ is an advancing process, Schwenckfeld taught a *progressive* justification, sanctification, and regeneration. To the extent that the Christian participates in Christ, to that degree is he justified, sanctified, and reborn (XII, 370). The entire new man, then, proceeds toward an ever fuller participation in Christ and the divine nature.

Together with contemporary reformers, Schwenckfeld considered the doctrine of justification the supreme theological concern of his day as well as the *"Summa Euangelij Christi et doctrinae Christianae"* (XIII, 867). But his understanding of justification bore little resemblance to that of Luther and the other reformers. Undoubtedly the broadest of his day, Schwenckfeld's definition of the term comprehended the entire soteriological process:

> *Iustificatio*, the justification or making-righteous of the sinner, is God's gracious action with man for his blessedness from beginning to end, by which the sinner is converted, reborn, made pious, righteous, holy, and finally blessed.... For *Iustificare* here [in St Paul] is actually nothing else than to make righteous and God-pleasing, to renew, regenerate, and make a child of God and heir of the kingdom of heaven.[1]

From 1528 on Schwenckfeld became increasingly opposed to the view of justification identified with Wittenberg. He asserted that justification is not a declarative, juridical, forensic, or imputative act of God, a mere forgiveness and non-imputation of sins, a *justificatio impii*; but rather the communication and inculcation of an essential righteousness within the believing human heart, stemming from the indwelling

---

[1] XIV, 791; cf. also XIII, 867.

of Christ.[1] The righteousness which justifies "...is the Lord Christ himself, who has become for us wisdom, righteousness, sanctification, and redemption, and now dwells in the heart of the believing, new, reborn man" (XII, 196).

Although Schwenckfeld usually assigns the mode of justification to the indwelling person of Christ, the Lord's interior presence also occasions the justifying inhabitation of the Holy Spirit (XII, 370) and, ultimately, the Trinity itself (XII, 885). In his nearly christomonistic theology, however, Schwenckfeld usually holds to Christ, Word and glorified flesh, as the characteristic Justifier.

Possessed of his Lord's righteousness, the believer is not merely declared righteous by God, but is, in fact, essentially righteous:

> God accounts no one righteous in whom nothing at all of his essential righteousness is found. Therefore they ["the scholars of God"] so seek justification or righteousness through faith in Christ that it not only is imputed to them or remains outside of them, but that they genuinely, essentially, truly, and perceptively participate in the righteousness of Christ in their soul, heart, and conscience; that through the reigning King of grace, Jesus Christ, and his Spirit, they become reborn, pious, righteous, and new men (XII, 458).

Essential righteousness, then, proceeds from the subjective experience of Jesus' indwelling presence in the believer. The Christian must not only have faith that God forgives his sins, but his conscience must be

---

[1] VIII, 768· "Imputatiua Iustitia ist nit genug hieher/ sonder es muss vera & essentialis Dei iustitia sein/ (welche Christus ist/ I. Cor. 1./ die uns vor Gott gerecht mache." Cf. also III, 890; VIII, 768, 823, 844-49; IX, 849, XII, 370-73; 973. To be sure, as with many of Schw.'s doctrines, some passages can be found which indicate the converse, in this case, an imputative justification. Where Schw. stresses the suffering and death of Christ and then makes the soteriological application to the Christian, Luther's doctrine of justification is sometimes approached, and a species of imputed righteousness is often accorded the believer. This, however, usually applies only to the Christian who is already righteous by essential justification. To such an individual God does not *impute* the sins which remain in his person out of weakness, cf. V, 366-373, 396. Clearly the basic difference lies in Schw.'s broad understanding of justification, which includes sanctification and the entire *ordo salutis*, as we have seen. By definition, therefore, justification cannot remain extrinsic to the believer, even if the ultimate cause of this justification is the objective *Leistung* of Christ. For this work must, in Schw.'s definition, be applied to men. According to the necessities of his system, then, justification had to be the ontological righteousness occasioned by the indwelling of Christ, and not merely an imputed righteousness. Therefore Albrecht Ritschl, *Die christliche Lehre von der Rechtfertigung und Versöhnung* (Bonn, 1883), is substantially correct, at least so far as the older Schw. is concerned, when he concludes, I, 319. "Schwenckfeld von einer angerechneten Gerechtigkeit nichts wissen wollte." So also Baur, *Versöhnung, etc.*, p. 462, who asserts that Schw. places "an die Stelle der imputativen Gerechtigkeit die wesentliche." On the other hand, Hahn, *op. cit.*, pp. 61 ff., and Loetscher, *op. cit.*, 481 ff., seem to be trying to save Schw. for orthodoxy in some of their statements.

free of them; he must perceive the inner presence of Christ by the renewal of his person, the joy in his heart, and the peace of his soul. Having sensed the emanation of God's grace, he will battle against sin and defeat the flesh (X, 952, et passim). "This all, as stated, must genuinely be experienced, perceived, and felt by the elect, each in his measure, here in the time of grace; even as with the damned God's anger and sin is sensed. For man is righteous on earth to the extent that he has in his heart the divine righteousness, which is Christ" (XII, 196).

The similarity between Schwenckfeld's concept of justification and that of Andreas Osiander of Nürnberg will have become apparent by now. Although the two were not on intimate terms – Osiander, indeed, declared, "Schwenckfeldt is wholly and truly possessed with the Devil" [1] – their concepts of justification did coincide to some extent. For his part, Schwenckfeld acknowledged that Osiander was closer to a correct interpretation of justification than Wittenberg [2] and approved his teaching of Christ's essential indwelling as the mode of justification in opposition to an imputative righteousness.[3] Nevertheless, he offered the following criticism of Osiander's doctrine:

> That Osiander, however, regards Christ only according to his divinity or divine nature as our righteousness and excludes his incarnation in the work of justification I consider incorrect. This means dividing Christ in the office of justification as much as if one would say that he were our righteousness only according to his humanity or human nature (XIII, 873).

According to Schwenckfeld, Osiander's error stemmed from two christological misconceptions: a failure to regard Jesus as the natural son of God according to both natures, and considering the humanity of Christ a creature even in glory (XIII, 876). Schwenckfeld also objected to Osiander's understanding of faith. The Nürnberger had written that the believer's present righteousness could not rest on the redemption which Jesus had achieved for man by his passion and death

---

[1] MS. germ. 898, fol. 55, Berlin, Preuss. St. Bibliothek, as quoted in VIII, 131. Osiander charged that Schw. was responsible for the coming of the Interim.

[2] XV, 3. Naturally Schw. rejected the Wittenbergian concept of justification also after Luther's death, including the theologizing in opposition to Osiander's definition of justification. Schw. insisted that God inhabited the human heart *substantialiter*, not merely *effectiue* as Melanchthon, Amsdorf, and Jonas explained it. He also continued to take issue with Melanchthon's insistence that *justificare* in St. Paul meant *justum pronunciare* (XIII, 882 ff., 1000) and consisted essentially in the forgiveness of sin (XIV, 791). Flacius' concept of justification he condemned as a Judaizing attempt to seek righteousness on the basis of Christ's active obedience (XIII, 883).

[3] *Loc. cit.* Erbkam, *op. cit.*, p. 443, is mistaken in asserting without qualification that Schw. "Osianders Rechtfertigungslehre entschieden verwirft...."

some 1500 years before. Such a view of the redemption was too historical in Schwenckfeld's estimation and misunderstood the nature of justifying faith. That faith was not conditioned by time or space, but made the redemption an ever-present reality to the believer.[1]

Schwenckfeld's doctrine of justification will become clearer when it is viewed in conjunction with his concept of faith. Following Luther, he regarded the doctrine of justification by faith as the heart of the gospel (II, 57); but, with faith as with justification, the lay theologian would content himself only with a Schwenckfeldian and not a Lutheran definition. And because of his singular interpretation of justifying faith, we must conclude that Schwenckfeld's whole soteriology has an entirely different orientation from that of Wittenberg, despite some similarities with Luther in Christology. In this regard it must be remembered that Schwenckfeld's doctrine was the crystallization of a life-time of opposition to what he regarded as the truncated Lutheran gospel, a faith which failed to bear ethical fruit. His own concept of faith was correlated to a Christology which posited the glorified humanity of Christ as the object of faith, a soteriology which stressed the indwelling of that humanity, and an ethical concern for empirical sanctification.

In Schwenckfeld's estimation, Lutheran doctrine presented an external, historical, rationalistic faith which failed to coordinate either with Christ's internal, essential righteousness, or sanctification and the new man (II, 494-96, *et passim*). It had a false origin: a communication through the means of grace which Schwenckfeld denied (II, 495). It drew false comfort from external sources: from passages of Holy Scripture, for example, or from participation in the sacraments rather than in the glorified Lord (XII, 970 ff.). It had a false object: justifying faith did not rest on the fact of Jesus' having shed his blood for our redemption, but in the forgiveness available to the believer directly from the indwelling Lord (XII, 973). A purely Scriptural faith in Christ, therefore, was not a justifying faith:

> No one is righteous or blessed before God according to the faith and knowledge by which one merely believes that Christ is that which the Scriptures say concerning him. For otherwise all would have to be righteous and blessed who, according to the testimony of Holy Scriptures, have accepted Christ as their Redeemer and Sanctifier and are called Christians (XII, 373).

---

[1] XIII, 878. For Schw.'s full critique of Osiander's doctrine, see XIII, 872-79. Cf. also Baur, *Dreieinigkeit, etc.*, pp. 246 ff., and Hahn, *op. cit.*, pp. 63 ff.

The Lutheran concept was even wrong in ascribing a false essence to faith. For to Schwenckfeld, justifying faith was not merely knowledge, assent, and confidence in a historical and external promise of forgiveness, but, like the righteousness, sanctification, and regeneration which it communicated, faith was itself a substantial quality from the essence of God![1] Even *sola fide* in the Lutheran sense was also to be questioned.[2]

Schwenckfeld arrived at his unusual doctrine of faith directly through his concept of justification. If the believer is justified (*made righteous*) through the essential indwelling and ethical righteousness of Christ in the heart, by what means, manner, or mode does the glorified Lord enter the heart and justify man? How is the nexus established between Christ and the Christian? By faith, according to Schwenckfeld: "...true faith actually brings into the heart everything which

---

[1] See immediately *infra*. We cannot, therefore, but pass a negative judgement on the efforts of Ecke, *op. cit.*, p. 241, to approximate Schwenckfeldian and Lutheran soteriology, even that of the young Luther. "In der biblischen Lehre von der Aneignung des Heils waren beide Manner [Luth. and Schw.] gleichen Sinnes, ja Schwenckfeld verstand gerade in diesem Punkte Luther besser, als der Synergist Melanchthon und viele Lutheraner es vermochten." Although in the context Ecke proceeds to demonstrate their differences, it must be emphasized that especially in the "Aneignung des Heils" through justifying faith were Luther and Schw. on different planes. And since such fundamental soteriology is the heart of theology, Sippel's critique of Ecke, *op. cit.*, 963, is largely justified, as also his conclusion. "Dass Schwenckfeld innerlich mit Luther so gut wie nichts gemein hat, bedarf... keines Wortes."

[2] XII, 370 "*Lutherani* handeln Christum nur... *historicè, literaliter, carnaliter, cum sua sola Fide....*" In his earlier years Schw. never questioned the *sola fide*, e.g., III, 178: "...der rechte glaub... allein den menschen rechtfertiget und seliget/ on alle zuthun der werck/" Cf. also II, 45, 498; III, 878; V, 500. Later he scrupled the *sola* on technical grounds the word was not found in Scripture, and other divine benefits also made man righteous, such as the grace of God, he Holy Spirit, the Word of God, and the like (XII, 890). Doctrinally he opposed what he thought a complete dichotomy of faith and works in Lutheran theology and stated that while faith and works were not to be confused (II, 508), faith must be active and demonstrate itself in good works (II, 49, *et passim*) and a new life (IV, 861, *et passim*). He rejected work-righteousness (II, 51, 81; IX, 871, 877), although he did approach it in one passage, XII, 892: "Das aber nicht der blosse glaube wie sie daruon reden genugsam sey zum eingange ins reich der himmel/ sonder glaub und werck... das ist jnnerliche und eusserliche gerechtigkeit unzertheilig bey einander sein mussen/" Again, however, this is largely directed against the Lutheran *sola fide*. Ultimately, instead of *sola fide* Schw. preferred the formula: "Ja Christus durch den glauben in unserm hertzen wonende/ uns gerecht macht" (XII, 370), or "*Justificatio* kompt aussem erkantnus Christi/ durch den glauben/" (X, 707). Koyre, *op. cit.*, p. 3, therefore is excessive in stating: "*Sola fide salvemur* n'est pas plus luthérien que schwenckfeldien." On the other hand, only according to the Lutheran definition is Maron, *op. cit.*, p. 33, correct: "Das '*sola*' *fide* ist völlig ausser Kraft gesetzt." To his own pregnant definition of "*fide*" Schw. would surely append the "*sola*," cf. *infra*.

man believes. It makes it the heart's own and gives it as a possession, so that the believer can be sure of it before God." [1]

This could imply an instrumental function of faith analogous to its orthodox Protestant definition as a God-given ληπτικόν for apprehending divine grace and a rational, ethical, psychological acceptance of the gospel promise of forgiveness of sin. But this was not Schwenckfeld's understanding. He did agree that faith was a gift of God, but precisely for that reason it was something far greater than an intellectual-emotional-volitional reliance upon him. For "God, the kind and merciful Lord, confers nothing from himself and his heavenly essence upon men for the blessedness of their souls and for eternal life which is not his own, of his nature and essence, and what he is for himself" (XII, 885). Therefore faith, as God's gift *from* himself, is nothing less than part of the essence and nature *of* himself! The following is only one of many passages in which Schwenckfeld expounds his unusual, mysticallyaccented definition of faith:

> For true, genuine faith is fundamentally a gift of the essence of God, a little drop from the heavenly source-fountain, a little ray of the eternal sun, a small spark of the burning fire which is God himself, and, in short, an intercourse and participation in the divine nature.... For this reason is faith a gift of God, a present of the Holy Spirit, and, basically, one substance with him who gives and confers it [2]

---

[1] VII, 597. Cf. also IX, 717 "...alle die in Jesum Christum warhafftig gleuben/ den Herrn Jesum Christum/ nach der geistlichen warheit des glaubens/ mit seinem Leib/ Fleisch und Blut in jrem gleubigen hertzen haben/" Similarly, in XII, 885, faith brings the Trinity into the heart.

[2] X, 846. Schw.'s text reads. "Denn der rechte ware Glaub ist im grund ein gabe des wesens Gottes/ ein tropfflin des Himmlischen quellbronnens/ ein blicklin der ewigen Sonnen/ ein funcklin des brennenden Fewrs/ das Gott selber ist/ Und kurtzlich ein gemeinschafft und theilhafftigkeit des Göttlichen wesens/... Also ist nu der glaube ein gabe Gottes/ ein geschenck des heiligen Geistes/ Ein wesen im grunde mit Dem/ der jhn gibet und schencket...." For other such mystical definitions of faith, see II, 566; VII, 347 ff., 596 ff.; XII, 889. Elsewhere Schw. equates faith with the Holy Spirit, e.g., II, 506: "...weil der glaube ein Gottlicher streen aussem heiligen Geiste ja der heilige Geiste selbs und die innerliche krafft Gottes ist imm hertzen damit man die ewigen Guter inn Christo einnimpt." Again, in IV, 235, faith is the "stroum und glantz des gaists Gottes... damit wir biss in hymel hinauff fur den thron Gottes gezogen werden/ ....In Summa der recht glaub ist ain wesentliche ergreiffung/ summa und empfengknuss der gottlichen gerechtigkait/ weisshait und warhait/ welche nichts anders ist/ dann unser Herr Jesus Christus." To Schw. the object of faith transcends time and place, for it is Christ himself, VII, 347. "Der glaube ist... ein blicklin dess wesens/ darinn alles ewig und gegenwertig gesehen wird/ Drumb so fasset er Christum Gott und Menschen/ nicht in zeit/ stett und formen/ sonder ausser aller zeit und stett/ auch weil Er in zeit und stett alhie hat gewandelt/" Cf. also VII, 596 f. Wach, *op. cit*, p. 25, correctly calls Schw.'s definition of faith "...the closest approximation to a mystical concept in Schw.'s theology." *Vide infra* for further discussion of the mystical implications of Schw.'s concept of faith.

This definition, in Schwenckfeld's opinion, explains why such great things are predicated of faith in the New Testament. For this reason faith can move mountains, change old men into new, and produce good fruits. Why are believers called children of God? Because by faith they participate in his nature and essence, much as natural children possess the character and substance of their fathers (X, 846-48). Again, "...faith makes righteous. How can this happen? It is a small ingrafting of the divine righteousness implanted in the heart of man" (X, 847). Hence the complete competence of true faith for the entire soteriological process: "It is a salutary, perceptible power and participation in the essence of God, through which man is directly renewed, reborn, and entirely endued with a new nature and being" (VII, 350).

Schwenckfeld's definition of justifying faith is, indeed, consistent if he took his understanding of the mode of justification seriously, and he did. For faith attains the *inhabitatio Christi* as the *fundamentum justificationis* precisely because *faith is itself a part of Christ* and the divine essence. Fantastic as the concept appears at first blush, this spiritual-substantial interpretation of faith is but an ultimate conclusion of Schwenckfeld's system. One of the major burdens in his theology had been to demonstrate the immediacy of Christ and the Christian. Jesus himself was the only all-sufficient Mediator, and he took up his residence in the believing heart independent of all externals or means other than himself (III, 509; IV, 34, *et passim*). If faith, then, were also a means by which the essential presence of Christ was secured in the heart, it was precisely because faith was itself, in some part, Christ!

Schwenckfeld's doctrine of faith is also in harmony with his general soteriological theory: "Therefore God became man in order that man might become united with God, exalted in him, and participate in the divine essence, honor, and glory. That is the true Christian faith to which the Holy Scriptures testify, as they are also entirely oriented to this mystery" (V, 782). As human flesh had become glorified in Christ and coordinate with the Word in all soteriological functions, it could now, to a degree, become essentially present and conjoined through faith to the believer, who, in turn, realized some small participation in the divine nature by the very fact of faith itself! Through genuine faith, therefore, the humanity of Jesus could realize its soteriological function as the great catalyst in dissolving the dichotomy between God and man, "...for otherwise no flesh can be united with God, who is a spirit, without the mediation of the flesh of Christ." [1]

To summarize, according to Schwenckfeld's singular interpretation of the doctrine of justification by faith, the believer is *made righteous* through an *inhabitatio Christi in corde* attained by means of a substantial-spiritual faith, which, in turn, is partially its own object: Christ himself, Word and glorified flesh.[2]

A detailed exposition of Schwenckfeld's doctrines of sanctification and regeneration would essentially only restate what has already been discussed under justification. For not only did his broad definition of justification comprehend the entire *ordo salutis*, but where the separate stages of an *ordo* are listed, Schwenckfeld either coordinated and conflated these in his theologizing, or regarded them as parallel processes issuing from the same source, the *inhabitatio Christi*. For the spiritual-substantial presence of the glorified Lord *in corde* was ultimately the single cause and mode of the entire soteriological process according to Schwenckfeld. To be sure, this process is occasionally differentiated into an *ordo salutis* or *"Ordo Iustificationis,"* as, for example: *"Regeneratio, Viuificatio, Innouatio, Iustificatio, Diuinae nature participatio,"* [3] yet each of these phases is but a variation on the theme of Christ's indwelling activity in the heart.[4] Thus the *Christus inhabitans* addresses, converts, regenerates, vitalizes, redeems, renews, justifies, sanctifies, marries, baptizes, anoints, adorns, feeds, and perfects the believing heart, thereby enabling its participation in the divine nature and according it eternal life. Word and sacrament, therefore, are also particular functions of the indwelling Lord. The Eucharist is a spiritual nourishing of the heart and soul by the *Christus incordatus*. Baptism is an interior heart-washing and cleansing by the same Agent. The Word of God is the true gospel preached by Christ himself speaking in the soul, and the like.

---

[1] IV, 27. Cf. IV, 37 "Corpus Christi est Templum gratiae, non aliunde habetur Gratia, quem per carnem Christi, haec est vnicum canale, vnicum medium, per quod influit gratia Dei in credentes." Cf. also VII, 345, 792.

[2] Cf. XII, 899, where Schw. makes a quantitative, but not qualitative, distinction between faith and Christ.

[3] XIII, 885. Cf. IV, 171, where Schw. lists eight components of the *ordo salutis* "Erlosung, Widergeburt, Vermahlung, Tauffe, Salbung, Bekleidung, Nachtmal, Volkommenheit/ und das ewige Leben;" or X, 780 f., where fifteen stages of salvation are recorded, but these seem more pious phraseology than systematic categorization.

[4] Schoeps, *op. cit.*, p. 31, aptly remarks "Der Christus incordatus ist an die Stelle des Christus incarnatus getreten." Schw., however, would reply that the "Christus incordatus" is none other than the "Christus incarnatus vel glorificatus."

Similarly, true faith, as the spiritual-substantial apprehension of the glorified Lord, receives the *Christus inhabitans* and appropriates his benefits. For this reason Schwenckfeld freely equates faith with the reception of Christ, eating the body and blood of the Lord, being washed by him, incorporation into Christ, and participation in his nature and essence.[1] It should finally also be mentioned that, as with faith itself, Schwenckfeld considered righteousness, holiness, rebirth, renewal, etc. not as accidental qualities occasioned by Jesus' indwelling, but as substantial parts of the *Christus incordatus*![2]

It remains for us to examine the objectives of the *ordo salutis* in Schwenckfeld's system and the eschatology in his soteriology. It has been stressed repeatedly that he interpreted salvation as consisting in man's deliverance from sin and creaturity, and his participation in the divine nature. When, and to what extent were these objectives realized by the believer?

If Schwenckfeld's anthropology had very low respect for natural man, regarding him as a slave to evil who was separated ethically and ontologically from the divine nature, his soteriology had a very high estimate of the regenerate or new man. Indeed, he never tired of stressing, almost exaggerating the Pauline antithesis of the old and new man, the unregenerate and the regenerate. In contrast to the old, the new man is sinless before God (VII, 323; XI, 787), since he is regenerated by a quasi-reincarnation of the indwelling Christ (V, 425; VII, 424) and harbors in his heart not only the person of the glorified Lord, but also his attributes, including holiness and righteousness.[3] Sanctification is then the continuous crucifixion of the old nature with its sin and fleshly lust, and the progressive generation and growth of the new by means of the inhabitation of Christ (VI, 134). Schwenckfeld, however, was no perfectionist. He sanely acknowledged that the new man does not exclusively predominate in this life, but wages a constant battle with the old (IV, 697). Not until eternity would man's

---

[1] II, 571-74; III, 156; IV, 28; V, 678 f.

[2] XIII, 347; XIV, 455. Statements such as these occasioned the famous critique of Schwenckfeldian theology by Flacius, *Verlegung der kurzen Antwort des Schwenckfeldt* (1554), p. C iii "Was ist er aber fur ein toller Heiliger, dem das Wort Gottes das Wesen Gottes selbst ist, das Evangelium ist ihm das Wesen Gottes, der Glaube ist ihm das Wesen Gottes, unsere Erneuerung ist ihm das Wesen Gottes, unsere Gerechtigkeit vor Gott ist ihm das Wesen Gottes. Alle Gaben des heiligen Geistes sind ihm das Wesen Gottes."

[3] XIV, 455· "So stehet nun die theilhafftigkeit nicht allein inn seiner Personen gemeinschafft/ sondern in der gemeinschafft alles dess/ was Er vom Vater erblich ewigklich hat/ was Er auch inn seiner menscheit durch seinen gehorsam uns zu gut hat erworben/ das ist Gottes gnad/ leben/ gerechtigkeit/ heiligkeit/ das Gottliche wesen/ wonn und freude/ unnd die miterbschafft des Reichs der Himmel."

subjective apprehension of Christ's victory over sin be complete and his true humanity realized: "First in the resurrection, when sin is scratched out, will the human nature be genuine. Here it is hypocrisy and inconstancy." [1]

The extent of human liberation from creaturity forms a close parallel to Schwenckfeld's concept of the believer's deliverance from sin. He never stated that the Christian was ever fully emancipated from a status of creaturity in this life, for the Bible itself would contradict such a proposition: "If any one is in Christ, he is a new creation" (II Cor. 5 : 17). To the extent that a believer exists as the new man, however, he is not simply to be designated a creature without further qualification: "Not only is the word 'creature' not to be tolerated in the case of Christ, but, without further explanation, should be avoided also for the children of God, as is easily observed in I John 3" (VII, 566). Even if the denomination "new creature" satisfied Schwenckfeld as characterizing the regenerate, this expression was rather to be replaced by "child of God," since believers were the products of divine generative as well as creative activity.[2] According to the logic of Schwenckfeld's system, moreover, the *Christus incordatus* could even confer to the regenerate his attribute of non-creaturity.[3] Again, however, since regeneration – as justification and sanctification – is never perfect in this life, but progresses in proportion to the presence of Christ in the heart (XII, 370), the believer's full non-creaturity is relegated to the eschatological realm. Then first, having recapitulated a process completed in their divine Prototype, would Christians also lay aside their creaturely nature and be changed into new, heavenly beings. As in the case of Christ, however, the integrity of their true humanity in genuine bodies and souls would not be compromised (VII, 505).

The elimination of sin and creaturity constituted the negative preparation for that ultimate object of God's plan of salvation and of the *Erkenntnis* and *Inhabitatio Christi*: man's participation in the nature of God himself and the consequent realization of his own true humanity (IV, 680; XI, 424). This is the recurrent eschatological

---

[1] VII, 305. Cf. also VII, 764; IX, 983.

[2] VII, 545· "...nicht alles menschlich flaisch ist ein geschaffen flaisch/ Gott der Allmachtige kan auch durch andre weise ainen menschen oder fleisch herfur bringen weder durch die schopffung/ er ist nicht allein ein schopffer der Creaturen/ sonder auch ain vatter viler kinder/" Cf. also XIV, 320.

[3] Perhaps also ubiquity: cf. VI, 83, where Schw. states that even "new men" cannot be circumscribed in a corporeal place.

motif which pulsates through all of Schwenckfeld's Christology and soteriology, and, in fact, motivated much of his theology. Anchoring his eschatology to II Peter 1 : 4 ("...you may... become partakers of the divine nature"), he quoted the passage incessantly as if to defend the apparent presumption of so glorious an expectation.[1] He even regarded this hope of the believer as a prime argument for the deification of Christ's own humanity! [2]

How, when, and to what extent, according to Schwenckfeld, does the Christian share in the divine nature? This participation, just as the other components of the *ordo salutis* which prepare for it, is a progressive process proportional to the believer's faith: "All true Christians participate in the nature of Christ according to the measure of their faith" (XV, 275). True participation in the divine nature, therefore, begins already in this life:

> Yes, such grace did Christ... gain for us that all true believers in him not only have forgiveness of sins . but also, for Christ's sake (although still in the flesh of sin, still mortal, weak, and vile) participate abundantly in the divine essence, life, spirit, and nature already here on earth, as also is written in II Peter 1 (VI, 636).

> God gives his rich spirit to destitute men and makes them participants of his divine nature and essence here on earth through faith, in which they also grow and increase, yes, live and are maintained eternally. There is, however, no mixing of the spirit with the flesh, nor any extinguishing of the human nature by the nature of God; indeed it happens without any loss or diminution of God.[3]

Schwenckfeld thus limits temporal participation in the divine nature to the inner and spiritual part of the believer, specifically, his heart, soul, and conscience.[4]

Like total sinlessness and non-creaturity, complete participation in the divine will not occur until after the final resurrection and judgment. Because of the fact that the believer will assume a heavenly flesh and possess a glorified body, his participation in the divine nature will necessarily be much more thorough than on earth, where only the

---

[1] III, 889, VI, 126, 241, *et passim*.

[2] VII, 212: "Auss welchem allem leicht ist zuerkennen/ sintemahl die göttliche Natur in die Christgleubigen vonn Christo unnd durch Christum herkommet/ dass Er je von Natur Gott/ ja der naturliche Son Gottes sein muss/ Denn wo Er die gottliche Natur nicht als sein eigenthumb selbs het/ so wurden wir solche keines wegs auss gnaden inn jhm mogen erlangen."

[3] VII, 718; cf. also X, 697.

[4] II, 550; III, 148; IV, 31.

spirit is affected.¹ The saved will undergo a process of glorification similar to Christ's:

> Since the splendor, glory, and magnificence of the nature which God the Father has naturally given to Christ as his son will, out of his gracious mercy, be imparted also to all Christians, John 17, so very much depends on the knowledge of that glory in which Christ, as crowned king, rules today. It is most necessary that Christians earnestly search, intercede, and direct their faith thereafter, and eternally comfort themselves that they will participate in such glory.²

First in this exaltation when man shares in the divine nature will he have become *true* man, that is, one possessed of an immortal, stable, holy, incorruptible, illocal, and non-creaturely body (VII, 764-66).

While Schwenckfeld never precisely defined his understanding of human participation in the divine nature, several passages from his writings do have an unmistakeable pantheistic, if well-nigh Scriptural, ring: "All Christians become children of God through the man Christ, participants in the divine nature, and, as the Scriptures say, gods. For the whole Lord Christ can so dispose that they become entirely children of God and, as Christ himself says, gods" (VIII, 405). Again, "We also hope to be received up into the single, eternal Godhead through Christ" (VIII, 381). Similarly, I Corinthians 15 : 28 ("...that God may be everything to every one") is given the following interpretation by Schwenckfeld: "That we shall become wholly full of divine life and heavenly joy, blessedness, and essence, to the eternal saturation of grace; indeed that we shall even become gods. But this all through Jesus Christ, from whose fullness of the essence and glory of God all the members of his body are united with God, filled, and inhabited by him."³

Indeed, in this sense and with the proper understanding and limitations, one might use the term deification (*Gottwerdung*) in reference not only to Christ, but also to believers who become glorified

---

¹ Cf. VII, 762: "Also hoff ich armer durch ihn und von ihm gebessert/ ernewert/ auch gantz auffzusteen in ein unsterblich/ unuerrucklich wesen einzugehn/ und seiner glorien tailhafftig zu werden im ewigen leben/ nicht allein nach dem geist/ oder seelen/ sonder an leib/ fleisch/ blut/ seel/ geist und am gantzen menschen/" For Schw.'s high eschatological hopes in this connection, see esp. VII, 762-66.

² VII, 532; cf. also VI, 518 f.; VII, 525.

³ XII, 550 f. In another passage Schw. even identifies eternal life with the essence of God, VIII, 782: "...welche Gotheit aber wol dem das zeytlich ist mitgetheilt kan werden/ Wa blibe sonst das zeugknus Petri/ das wir Gotlicher natur durchs erkandtnus Christi theylhafftig werden. und Pauli/ das wir wachsen sollen zur grosse Gottes/ Ja wa blibe unser ewigs leben? Ists nit God selbst?"

through him.[1] Finally, Schwenckfeld even maintained that "man is to reign through Christ in God, for which reason Christ became man" (X, 698).

Small wonder that the reformer found himself accused of pantheism, or the making of plural gods (XI, 346). To refute the latter charge, he cited Psalm 82 : 6 and John 10 : 34 ff.[2] As to pantheism, Schwenckfeld tried to guard himself against anything approaching the doctrine. "All those who say that God is naturally and essentially in all creatures, here, there, and in everyone separately – which is also approximately what the heathen poets have said – impugn the honor and majesty of God."[3] As was observed, Schwenckfeld opposed Luther's ubiquity as pantheistic (III, 210, 218; XII, 936). He further rejected pantheistic passages in Zwingli (XII, 935), the philosophical pantheism of the Manichaeans (IV, 8), as well as Sebastian Franck's quasi-pantheistic teaching that a divine seed was implanted in the human heart from birth.[4] Pantheism, moreover, would have violated the very fundamental dichotomy upon which Schwenckfeldian theology had been erected: the ethical, ontological, separation between Creator and creature, spiritual and physical, inner and outer.

In this connection Schwenckfeld interpreted the omnipresence of God in a double sense. There is the *praesentia potentiae*, according to which God is present to all creatures and they to him because of his function in maintaining and preserving them – his true essence, however, remaining exterior to the creature; and the *praesentia gratiae*, in which God is peculiarly present to all believers, who are not excluded from the divine essence, but rather participate in it by virtue of divine regeneration through the indwelling of Christ.[5]

Would not, then, the gracious union of God with the believer through the indwelling of Christ imply a particular or "selective" pantheism in which all the regenerate, but not all men, were included?

---

[1] IX, 682 f.; *vide infra*, however, for the qualifications which Schw. makes in this regard.

[2] "I say, 'You are gods....'" *Loc. cit.*

[3] II, 537; cf. also IV, 5; V, 499-501.

[4] V, 422 f.; VI, 45; VII, 152; VIII, 469. Baur, "Mystik, etc.," 523, is inaccurate in stating that according to Schw.: "Der Mensch hat an sich ein göttliches Princip in sich, und kann daher aus der Endlichkeit seiner geschaffen Natur zur Unendlichkeit seines wahren göttlichen Wesens sich erheben." This is, rather, the doctrine of Franck.

[5] IV, 6 f. "Es sind die Creaturen also geschaffen/ dass sie ausswendig dem göttlichen wesen stehen sollen/ Allein der gleubige Mensch kompt darein/ in welchem auch allein Gott wesentlich und natürlich/ durch die widergeburt/ die da geschucht in Christo Jesu/ wonet." Cf. also III, 210; XII, 935; XIV, 320.

To be sure, Schwenckfeld did delimit the indwelling of Christ to the believer and not to all men. But whether his understanding of this selective participation in the divine nature should be regarded as a pantheism in some sense is another question. Schwenckfeld never called it that. In fact, he erected several safeguards against a pantheistic interpretation of participation in the divine nature. In this life, for example, only the spiritual part of believing man, the new man, shares in the essence of God (VII, 718). Even in eternity there will be a quantitative – although not qualitative – distinction between the glory of Christ and that of the believer:

> There is a great difference between the adopted children and the natural son of God, between the splendor of Christ and all the elect in Christ. There is, indeed, one kind of splendor, essence, glory, and magnificence in Christ and all his Christians. But in Christ, our Head and Lord, the ineffable total abundance of splendor is of the very highest grade with God his father.... Thus it is intolerable for his honor that he should be called our *Coheres* or co-heir (VII, 754).

Again, Schwenckfeld would permit no diminution of the "many great differences" between Jesus, as Son of God, and Christians, as adopted sons of God (IX, 297; XI, 351). Since the exalted humanity of Christ was the source of the believer's glorification, that humanity was necessarily more radiant than the glory it effected. The members must always accord the Head precedence in perfection (IX, 682). On this account and to avoid misunderstanding, Schwenckfeld preferred to reserve the term "apotheosis" for Christ alone, rather than applying it also to the Christian.[1]

Such a concept of the believer's participation in God, therefore, could not brook pantheism. On earth the scope of this divine-human communion was limited to the heart and soul of the Christian; and in glory, while the whole man would share in the divine nature, there would ever be a quantitative difference in the extent of Christ's participation in divinity and glory and that of the believer. The damned, moreover, had no such participation.

But what of Jesus' indwelling union with the believer? Here we are dealing not with a "selective pantheism," but with the *unio mystica* of Christ and the Christian. It becomes our final task to investigate the specific nature of the believer's apprehension of, and union with, his Lord – unquestionably, the holiest ground in Schwenckfeldian theology. Only then can we hope to answer the question, posed

---

[1] IX, 682 f.. "Drumb so wollest bedencken/ Ob solchs nicht auch/ der schwachen halben mocht gemildert werden/ das wir Apothosin/ noch zur zeit allein bey Christo lassen bleiben." Schw. also felt that the term "Gottwerdung" might greatly offend his opponents, *loc. cit.*

in every research into Schwenckfeld, as to whether or not the Silesian reformer was a mystic.

Probably no word in the vocabulary of theology is used with greater imprecision than "mysticism." Because of the widely-varying definitions of the term, Schwenckfeld has variously been classified as a non-mystic, a Protestant-Lutheran mystic, an intellectual mystic, a theoretical mystic, an ethical mystic, a pantheistic mystic, a Biblicistic-gnostic mystic, and an Anabaptist mystic.[1] Let us discuss briefly the possible mystical elements in the Schwenckfeldian system.

The importance of the German mystics in Schwenckfeld's theological development has already been noted; however he was not weaned on their writings, and when, after 1530, he did devote greater attention to the mystics, it was not without a critical eye. The *Theologia Germanica*, for example, was given only a guarded recommendation by the reformer: "It is high and deep, and I wish that Christ were named more often therein."[2] Again, when asked about the "Franckforter's" work, Schwenckfeld suggested: "I would advise you to hold yourselves to the brighter light and to the Holy

---

[1] According to Wach, *op. cit.*, p. 4: "Schwenckfeld is not a mystic, at least not in the narrower sense of this much abused term." So also Reinhold Seeberg, *Lehrbuch der Dogmengeschichte*, IV (Leipzig, 1917), 32: "Er [Schw.] ist weder Wiedertaufer noch auch eigentlich Mystiker gewesen...." Similarly Heinrich Bornkamm, "Mystik, Spiritualismus, und die Anfange des Pietismus im Lutherthum," *Vortrage der theologischen Konferenz zu Giessen*, Folge 44 (1926), 11, speaks of "...so unmystischen Gestalten wie Schwenckfeld." Per contra – Borngraber, *op. cit.*, p. 22, terms Schw. "...praktisch wie spekulativ der erste Vorkampfer der Mystik des 16. Jahrhunderts." Erbkam, *op. cit.*, p. 358, asserts: "Er ist nemlich unverkennbar ein entschiedener Repräsentant der intellektuellen Mystik;" on pp. 473 f. he even states that Schw. had attained "...den Hohepunkt protestantischer Mystik in dieser Zeit." Dorner, *Geschichte, etc.*, p. 176, characterizes Schw. as "...der edelste Repräsentant der theoretischen Mystik im Reformationszeitalter." Baur, "Mystik, etc.," 502, claims: "...er, wenn irgend einer der altern Zeit, ist der Repräsentant der protestantischen und zwar ganz besonders der protestantisch-lutherischen Mystik." He asserts that Schw. was "...ein ächt lutherischen Mystiker darin, dass ihm sein mystischen Bewusstsein ganz in der Anschauung der Person Christi ruhte," 510. Sippel, *op. cit.*, 927, concludes that Schw. reconstructed his theology "...zu einer eigenartigen Repristination der Gedanken der hellenistischen Mystik." Maron, *op. cit.*, p. 173, maintains that Schw.'s was a "biblizistisch-gnostisierende Mystik." Moreover, in the catalogues of significant mystics in church history, Schw. is often grouped with Tauler, Seuse, Bernard, Ruysbroeck, the Friends of God, Franck, and Weigel, as, e.g., in Adolf Köberle, *Rechtfertigung und Heiligung* (Leipzig, 1929), pp. 18 f. Others, however, have made entirely false estimates of Schw.'s mysticism, as, e.g., Thomas M. Lindsay, *A History of the Reformation* (New York, 1950), II, 422 f., who categorizes Schw. as an exponent of "pantheistic mysticism," an ideology which "...had no conception whatever of religion in the Reformation sense of the word." Lindsay wrongly makes of Schw. a secularly-minded philosopher, mistakenly calls him "an Anabaptist mystic," 456.

[2] IX, 319 f. Schw. probably read the *Theologia Germanica* first in 1545.

Scriptures...."[1] The *Imitatio Christi*, on the other hand, he valued above the *Theologia* and probably brought out an edition of a Kempis' (?) work at Augsburg in 1531 (IV, 264 ff.). Its theme of the cross as ethical example made a lasting impression on the theologian's life and thought. Some slight influence from Staupitz and Carlstadt may also be deduced from Schwenckfeld's publishing *Von der Gelassenheit* in 1538 (VI, 1 ff.), and an edition of Staupitz' *Ein seligs newes Jar/ von der lieb gottes* in 1547 (X, 732 ff.). The term resignation (*Gelassenheit*) appears consistently in Schwenckfeld's writings after 1530.

One of the more determinative influences on Schwenckfeldian theology, however, and certainly the most important mystical impulse derived from the writings of Johannes Tauler. Schwenckfeld read Tauler perhaps as early as 1524 (XII, 141) but probably not with any intensity until 1531 and thereafter.[2] He studied him critically, to be sure, maintaining that the theologian was not correct on all points because of his "papistic yoke" (XII, 554) and should therefore be read with caution (XI, 594). Nevertheless, Schwenckfeld absorbed not a few fundamentals of his theology from Tauler's pen and frankly acknowledged his indebtedness to the mystic. He asserted that through him he had learned to distinguish the spiritual gifts from the physical signs or ceremonies in the "acts of God" (XII, 141). Indeed, if Tauler was not – as he may well have been – responsible for Schwenckfeld's sundering the spirit from the letter, he, together with Cyril and Neo-Platonic elements in patristic writings, exercised the greatest influence on the reformer's rejection of an external means of grace and the erection of his theological dualism.[3]

---

[1] IX, 360 ff. Schw. also stated that when the *Theologia* dealt with *Gelassenheit*, hope, and eternal blessedness, it was very profitable; however "...sonst laufft vil fantaseij mit unter... das... mehr versterlich meines achtens/ denn besserlich ist/ lasst uns beij der einfallt der h. schrifft bleiben/"

[2] XII, 554. For the earliest refs. to Tauler, see I, 252, 389; II, 584; III, 86.

[3] Cf. other passages where Schw. cites Tauler as opposing an external means: VII, 445, 748; VIII, 404; XII, 500. In XI, 594, Schw. was accused of speaking "Platonice und Taulerisch" concerning the means of grace. In 1555 Schw. also edited Tauler's "Eyn trostliche Christenliche underweisung unnd verstand des eusserlichen und jnnerlichen worts Gottes," XIV, 349 ff., which reads like a textbook on Schwenckfeldian theology. Cf., furthermore, Tauler's influence on Crautwald, III, 86. The Christology of the mystic was also cited by Schw. as supporting the soteriological efficacy of Christ's flesh, cf. X, 437 and Tauler, *loc. cit.* Schw. likewise referred to Tauler's frequent use of the term "vergotten," XI, 920. Other elements in the mystic's theology also strike one as very "Schwenckfeldian" indeed, viz.: the immediacy of God and the inner man; Christ speaking in the believing soul; spiritual discernment in the sacraments; the use of John 6 to explain the Lord's Supper; within the dualism of internal and external, the retention of a certain function for externals; the exhortation to study Scripture as pointing

In the question of Schwenckfeld's possible mysticism, a consideration of the mystical content of his system itself is more important than the problem of his historical connection with, and indebtedness to, the German mystics. That a few elements in Schwenckfeldian theology are genuinely mystical by every reasonable definition of the term it would be idle to deny. His definition and doctrine of faith are rife with mystical overtones, and other suggestions of mysticism in his system will also have become apparent by now. The very origin of Schwenckfeld's theology as an opposition of the spirit to the letter and a determined protest against religious externalization parallels the inner, experiential, "heart" religion of the mystic in his reaction to similar conditions in church history. With all the important mystics, both Christian and non-christian, Schwenckfeld shared a basic conviction: the external was to be subordinated to the internal, the flesh to the spirit, the objective to the subjective. Indeed, as we have observed, he expanded this subordination into a massive dualism after the fashion of Neo-Platonic mysticism. The Schwenckfeldian diminution of the flesh, the body, and the creature as extraneous to God is axiomatic for mystical theology as well. On the other hand, the glorification of man and particularly his participation in the divine nature also closely parallel the eschatology of the mystics. Schwenckfeld's use of the term *Gelassenheit* and his references to the knowledge, perception, and, occasionally, vision (*Schau*) of God as well as an ascent to him, betray mystical overtones.

Whether or not Schwenckfeld is a genuine mystic, however, must be ascertained from the heart and aim of his soteriology: participation in Christ. For if the reformer is a mystic, his mysticism, as his entire religion and theology, centers in the union of the Christian and his indwelling Lord. In effect, we must ask Schwenckfeld for all the sacred details involved in that final stage and object of the *Erkenntnis Christi*: the *inhabitatio Christi*.

As previously observed, faith can effect the indwelling of Jesus primarily because it is itself a spiritual-substantial part of the divine essence of Christ. For the believer this means that faith is something preter-rational – a concept proven, yet guarded by Schwenckfeld's insistence that faith and knowledge must go side by side (II, 578) – an apprehension of the glorified Lord which must be *experiential*. The

---

to Christ; a denouncing of the ethics and the clergy of his day; faith as Christ himself, or an emanation from God; regeneration through an *inhabitatio Christi*; the Incarnation as God's becoming man so that man could become like God; man's eschatological goal as glorification and participation in the divine nature; and a stress on the *Erkenntnis Dei et Christi*.

believer must sense, perceive, discern the presence of Christ in his heart.[1] What, according to Schwenckfeld, is the precise nature of this experience? What, practically, is involved when Christ indwells the heart of the believer, unites with him, and communicates to him his divine flesh? Schwenckfeld never ventured any systematic exposition of the *inhabitatio Christi*, although his writings are replete with its description.

In the first place, such an experience can occur only in the heart of the regenerate because it alone, of all creation, is capable of being spiritualized and thereby providing an appropriate residence for the Word. The heart, then, constitutes the nexus between the human and the divine.[2] Elsewhere Schwenckfeld lists "soul, heart, and conscience" as areas peculiar to this divine-human concourse.[3] The Christian's activity in apprehending and appropriating the glorified Lord he defined as a very interior process:

> Each man must seek often and well after the inner visitation of God's grace in this manner: he must go into the innermost recess of his heart and there seek God the Lord essentially... correctly apprehending his son, Christ Jesus. In the obedience of faith he must become entirely united with him, so that, with the prophet, he may silently hear what the Lord, the eternal Word, speaks in him (X, 439).

This confrontation of Christ and the believer within the human heart takes place beyond the confines of space and time, and the phraseology of a mystic ascent is unmistakeable:

> The Christ-believing soul or heart is conveyed above itself through the spirit of faith beyond all time and place, and becomes attached to Christ, true God and man It is bound to and united with him, completely fed and nourished by him with his body and blood in heavenly being, not only according to one nature, but also according to the other (IV, 37).

Faith, again, in bringing the flesh and blood of the glorified Lord into the heart, draws the heart beyond itself into Christ and his exalted state. The believing heart is, in fact, heaven (IV, 31 ff., 138).

It will be noted that here is precisely the phraseology which Schwenckfeld employed in portraying his spiritual concept of the sacraments. In fact, most of the passages which best demonstrate

---

[1] II, 494; IV, 222. In XI, 886, Schw. speaks of a true faith "...der on empfindlichkeit nicht sein kann." Cf. also V, 363, where the same is predicated of justification and blessedness.

[2] II, 344 f.. "...non enim potest alligari Verbum Dei, Deus incarnatus rei externae, Quia Spiritus est & vita... non est igitur panis vllus capax Verbi viuificantis, neque potest fieri spiritalis per Verbum id, quod requiritur ad habitaculum Verbi, sed solum cor hominis fidele, quod verbum ipsum viuificauit." Cf. also II, 345, 489, 504; III, 135, 148; IV, 31, *et passim*.

[3] II, 550, 554; III, 148.

whatever mystical inclinations he may have possessed deal with the spiritual communication of Christ's exalted body and blood in the Silesian spiritual interpretation of the Eucharist. If the doctrine of the Lord's Supper first made a theologian of Schwenckfeld, it was the mode of Christ's nourishing the believer with his glorified self which remained his favorite illustration of the means by which the Christian became savingly united with his Lord: "He [Christ] draws the believing heart away from everything which is against and opposed to him, out of this earthly being and mode, beyond itself, to himself and in himself, into another essence – the spiritual, heavenly essence – in which he gladdens, feeds, fills, and satiates it with his divine grace and with the bread of eternal life." [1] The true celebration of the Eucharist, therefore, takes place "...beyond all time, place, and locality in God and in heaven" (VI, 160). For this reason Schwenckfeld could even make the seemingly fantastic statement that the believing, new man is not locally circumscribed, but, in communing with his Lord, is already translated into a heavenly being.[2]

Schwenckfeld preferred to speak of the very personal experience of communion with Christ only with close friends:

> Ask the Father and believe firmly that Christ wishes to feed and strengthen you, that is, to transform [*verwandeln*] you into himself so that he be in you and you in him, and do not question how or when, in what way or manner this transpires. For reason cannot perceive it; it is too high for it. But rather stand fast and wait in faith . The more rigorously you dismiss all creaturely aids, the sooner you will be helped. Faith directs itself to where nothing appears. Therefore, as soon as you are reminded in faith through the outer word, then immediately dismiss everything, look to the Father in secret, stand still there as long as you can, persisting with constant prayer, and believe that Christ must become food for you.... And when you have been fed by him, you do not live any longer, but he in you. Then one can truly say that the eater has been transformed into the food (V, 468).

> Especially, however, when you pray in the Lord's Prayer for daily bread, that is, for the supernatural bread of the soul, you should stop at this petition and, with cordial sighing, perceive if the Lord would feed your languishing soul.... Call also on the Lord Jesus that he would graciously dispense his flesh and blood, which is the bread which he gives (John 6),

---

[1] III, 506; cf. also II, 539 ff., 571 ff.; V, 205.

[2] VI, 83: "Seittenmal dann auch die Kinder des reichs/ das ist die newen menschen mit kainer leiblichen stelle mugen umgeschriben werden/ sie seind schon versetzt mit Christo nach der warhait des glaubens jns himlische wesen/ da halten sy mit irem kunig Christo sein herrlichs nachtmal essen von seinem leib und blute zum ewigen leben."

that the whole Christ, God and man, may become your food and full satiation, indeed, the single refreshment of your heart. Do not stop imploring until such a thing happens. Then your heart will brim with joy in thanksgiving, your eyes will run with tears, your mouth will overflow with praise, and your entire person will be filled with grace from God (VIII, 228).

The means by which man approaches God to be nourished by him, then, is confident prayer, or, as Schwenckfeld usually terms it, an "earnest prayer of faith" (X, 1032 ff.). "For through prayer the heart of man is conducted above itself into heaven and unto God" (IV, 704). Elsewhere this prayer of faith assumes a nearly mystical character.[1]

Other passages also demonstrate that Schwenckfeld felt himself in very close personal contact with God, but the phraseology in these can be attributed as much to his piety as to his mysticism (e.g., IV, 776 f.).

If, indeed, Schwenckfeld is a mystic, his is a contained mysticism. Because he sensed the enthusiasm and subjectivity implicit in any claim of immediate communion between God and the believer, Schwenckfeld set certain boundaries to guard the authenticity of the experience of the *inhabitatio Christi*. Although the Christian should at all times listen for the voice of God speaking in his heart, whether in church or at home (IV, 229, 776), he must nevertheless carefully determine if all such stirrings and utterances actually come from God (V, 693). For this reason Schwenckfeld did not stress the normativity of an immediate, contemporary revelation as did Münzer or Carlstadt. Similarly, when seeking God within the innermost reaches of his heart, the believer is not to "...sit down and wrap a coat over his head" (X, 439). Schwenckfeld neither regarded a life of detached contemplation as the Christian ideal, nor defined worship as an idle awaiting of the Spirit. Finally and most significantly, he was by no means the esoteric mystic who would uncharitably repudiate the unenlightened for not sharing in a recondite religious experience. An Elizabeth Hecklin once wrote the reformer that she feared God's wrath lest she be unable to comprehend the full knowledge of Christ in all his divine majesty. Schwenckfeld answered her that such a thought was *Anfechtung*. The Christian should certainly direct his attention to the love, mercy, and grace of Jesus also in his earthly existence (XII, 769). He himself confessed that his teaching concerning the glorified Lord was "too strong a food" for many. Such should always turn back

---

[1] Cf. X, 983, 1032 f. Prayer itself is sometimes given a quasi-mystical definition, e.g., X, 1011. "Und ist namlich das gebet ein erhebung der glaubigen seel/ oder auffsteigen des gemuts inn Gott inn himmel/ entzweder mit dancksagung umb seine wolthat/ oder mit ernsthafftem enhalten von Got etwas zuerlangen."

to the "milk-teaching" of an earthly and historical Christ (IX, 500).

To conclude our estimate of Schwenckfeld's mysticism, we must finally know what he regarded as indications that union with Christ had been effected, as well as the evidences of divine indwelling. The distinguishing marks of the *inhabitatio Christi* which Schwenckfeld lists are not ecstatic sensations of fusion with, or absorption into, God. Even emotional demonstrations are not unduly emphasized. Rather, the typical, Biblical "fruits of the Spirit" assure the believer that he has apprehended the glorified Lord and experiences his indwelling: "What does it mean that Christ is in us than that the kingdom of God, the righteousness of God, security of faith, peace, joy, grace, salvation, blessedness, and a good conscience are in us?" (V, 617). Other indications include: penitence over sin; battle against the flesh and old man; growth in grace; fervent prayer; inner possession of the power, love, and fear of God; forgiveness of sin; a spiritual foretaste of eternal life, and the like.[1]

It is also significant that Schwenckfeld never claimed or reported any special mystical trances, ecstasies, or transporting experiences other than the moments of deep devotion already cited.[2] And these, we may conclude, are not unbecoming to the reformer's gentle piety, wholesale consecration, and sense of fellowship with God. It may well be argued that, according to the needs of his system, Schwenckfeld *should* have experienced moments of sublime, ecstatic, mystical communion with his Lord were he actually apprehending his deified humanity with all the exalted magnificence Schwenckfeld had devoted his life to describe. But we have no record of any great mystical rapture of this kind in the *Corpus Schwenckfeldianorum*. Moreover, Schwenckfeld himself defined faith as but "...a little ray of the eternal sun" (X, 846), and the experience of participation in Christ was necessarily only very partial in this life: "If the Lord Christ inspires us poor, weak creatures with the smallest little glimpse of his love,

---

[1] IX, 314 f. Schw. lists identical spiritual tokens for determining whether or not the Christian has partaken of the spiritual Eucharist, VIII, 228. "So offt der Mensch empfindet Gottliche sussigkeit in Christo/ trost/ freud/ liebe/ gnad und barmhertzigkeit/ so offt Er einen vorschmack des ewigen Lebens hat/ so hellt er mit dem Herren sein Nachtmal." Similar terminology, moreover, is used to authenticate spiritual baptism, the hearing of the inner Word, the establishment of God's spiritual kingdom, and participation in the divine nature, IX, 859; X, 697.

[2] As previously noted, however, Schw. did make a claim for particular revelation, even if he never stressed this assertion, cf. XIV, 391 f., 945; XVI, Doc. MCLXVI. Nor did Schw. define the nature of the revelation in any precise manner. He was likely referring to his entire theology with its emphasis on the glorified Christ and his inner appropriation.

grace, and benefits, we are blessed, have escaped his wrath, and become children of grace." [1]

We should therefore summarize this discussion by granting the fact that Schwenckfeld was, indeed, a mystic. With a system which demanded the subjective apprehension and appropriation of the glorified humanity of Christ as *the* soteriological necessity, he could not be otherwise. But his was not a philosophical, speculative, or pantheistic type of mysticism which sought to grasp the essence of God by rational ascent into an impersonal and infinite divinity. Schwenckfeld's was rather a deeply religious mysticism, for its object was a practical communion with a personal God through his glorified Son. It called for an experiential participation, to some small degree, in the divine nature through the indwelling of Christ, and accordingly, was nothing more or less than a "Christ-mysticism" based predominantly on the Scriptures.

But if Schwenckfeld's was a Scriptural type of mysticism, probably none of his contemporaries places such a literal emphasis on the *sedes mysticae* in the New Testament as he. Paul's concept of the indwelling of Christ, John's portrayal of the children of God, and Peter's promise of participation in the divine nature were far more than word pictures for Schwenckfeld. True faith rendered them genuine realities! Thus did *die Teilhaftigkeit Christi*, participation in Christ, become the supreme object of Schwenckfeld's soteriology and the ultimate stage of *die Erkenntnis Christi*.

---

[1] XII, 769. Cf. XII, 889, where Schw. makes a quantitative, although not qualitative, distinction between faith and Christ: "...der glaube nit der gantze Christus/ noch die volle Christi und des h. Gaists ist." Cf. also XIV, 998.

CHAPTER XII

CONCLUSION

To evaluate Schwenckfeldian theology with necessary objectivity is to dispense with the usual categories of its criticism, i.e., either sweeping condemnation or spirited vindication. If Luther and other reformers are now being spared these alternatives, the time of moderation has come for Schwenckfeld as well.

A negative critique of Schwenckfeldian theology, to be sure, would be at no pains to discover certain minor inconsistencies and major areas of vulnerability. Besides those specifically cited in the text, Schwenckfeld's application of the doctrine of the Trinity might be questioned. The objection is possible that in his nearly christomonistic theology the functions peculiar to the Holy Spirit, according to orthodox Pneumatology, are assigned to the humanity of Christ. In fact, as we have noted, in several passages Schwenckfeld even identifies the Holy Ghost with the flesh of Christ.[1]

Again, the dualism which underlies the Schwenckfeldian system betrays a gnostic-like phobia for the natural and the external, and although the reformer struggles to maintain a rationale for externals, the unmistakeable stress in his theology is a consistent diminution of the outer man and the means by which he is reached: the church, the ministry, the sacraments, and, to an extent, even the Bible itself. If, then, we accept as a fact that the outer man has little crucial significance in Schwenckfeld's theology, an obvious discrepancy is his near-Donatistic emphasis on the necessary piety of both celebrant and communicants, his observance of a sacramental *Stillstand*, the appeal for a ban, strict ecclesiastical discipline, and the like. This but indicates the inner tensions in Schwenckfeld. While theoretically externals were clearly secondary in his system, Schwenckfeld's ethical consciousness preserved for them a definite significance in practice. His piety, then, was considerably more orthodox than his systematics. Our specific concern, however, is with the doctrine of the person and work

[1] XII, 398, cf. also V, 595, IX, 889.

of Christ. Accordingly, this discussion with Schwenckfeld will necessarily be limited to these *loci*.

As regards his Christology, the dogmatician would demand clarification on several important theologoumena, such as the ancestry of Jesus, the nature of the spiritual-yet-physical transmission of his flesh, and the progressive growth of Christ's humanity into divinity during his earthly ministry. But these are secondary to the two problematical *nova* in the Schwenckfeldian system: the non-creaturity of Christ, and the total deification of his humanity in glory.

Probably the most acute criticism of Schwenckfeld's doctrine of Jesus' non-creaturity was the soteriological argument of his opponent, Coccius,[1] which finds repetition in F. C. Baur:[2] if Christ had not assumed true creaturely flesh, he could neither be the savior of creaturely humanity, nor its mediator, brother, and representative before God. Schwenckfeld countered most potently that Christ, then, must also have been a sinner were he to save man from sin (IX, 1006).

Schwenckfeld's rejection of the term "creature" as a designation for Christ, however, is assailable from other viewpoints. The creaturely flesh of the Virgin Mary certainly contributed to the conception of Jesus, and it is difficult to see how even a generative – rather than creative – act of God could, or indeed would find it necessary to, alter the plain physical fact of the creaturity and continuity of that flesh. To the argument of the special circumstances of Christ's conception can be opposed that of his genuine humanity, which, if circumscribed by terrestrial limitations in the state of humiliation, should have found a *status creaturae* not essentially inconsonant. And the fact that a true human flesh which ate and slept should also have been creaturely does not by any means, as Schwenckfeld sensed implicitly, militate against the holiness of that flesh. Ultimately, any compromising of the fact that God became creaturely in Christ is a diminution of the miracle of the Incarnation.

But Schwenckfeld would not be balked at such criticism. As we have seen, he conceded that in the state of humiliation Jesus might, indeed, be designated a "new creature." And, certainly, no theological

---

[1] IX, 978· "Hat er [Jesus] eyn ander nit warhafftig geschaffen menschen fleysch an sich genommen/ wie Schwenckfeld sagt/ so hat er auch eyn ander/ nit das warhafftig geschaffen menschen fleysch erloset. Hat er eyn ander fleysch erloset/ dann unser fleysch/ so bleibt/ und ist unser fleysch eyn unerloset fleysch/ und sein/ unnd bleiben wir der sund/ des tods/ und des teuffels eygen." On this occasion, Schw. replied "Calumnia. Eitell Sophisterej. Das fleisch sollte und muste vil herrlicher sein das uns solte erlosen weder das geschaffne fleisch/ Nemlich Ein fleisch des Sunes Gottes."

[2] Baur, "Mystik," 515.

critique should take umbrage at such an epithet. The substance of Schwenckfeld's crusade for Christ's non-creaturity, however, referred to the state of exaltation. Here he actually understood the term "creature" more as an attribute of imperfection and servility than as a designation of origin. In the case of the glorified Lord, "creature" became nothing more or less than a term of opprobrium primarily because Schwenckfeld considered its connotations antithetical to his guiding concept of the exalted Christ. In this context, only a Nestorianizing Christology would stand irreconcilably hostile to Schwenckfeld's basic concern, stemming as it did from his connotative understanding of creaturity.

The companion doctrine of the deification of Christ's humanity was ultimately far more central to Schwenckfeld's theology and, in fact, constitutes his gospel. A critique here is necessarily double. On the one hand, the magnificence of Schwenckfeld's consistent, crusading, nearly-inspired fixation on the person of the glorified Christ must be acknowledged. On the other, the reality of Jesus' humanity in glory would seem hopelessly compromised, and the attempts of Schwenckfeld to salvage a true humanity for the exalted Lord certainly appear less than satisfactory. In this regard, however, the reformer is vulnerable only through his anthropology. For the Schwenckfeldian eschatological definition of man posits nothing less than participation in the divine nature as elemental for true humanity. The implication that this makes of contemporary man, especially the non-Christian, something sub-human is never explored by Schwenckfeld in any great detail.

A criticism of Schwenckfeld's doctrine of the work of Christ is inevitably that of the Christian West, with its practical soteriology based on psychological-ethical principles, against the Christian East, with its physical-hyperphysical conceptualization of salvation. For in many respects Schwenckfeld might be designated "the Irenaeus of the Reformation Era," the East's exponent in the West. Arguments for or against a theory of real redemption, however, are not specific to this study.

Nevertheless, in the dogma concerning the appropriation of salvation through faith, subjective soteriology, Schwenckfeldian doctrine appears unsatisfactory from several points of view. The Lutheran would particularly object to Schwenckfeld's concept of justification, which, with its particularistic and subjectivisitic emphasis, its stress on the moral rather than the religious, lacks the security and objective comfort of Luther's gospel, born of the *Anfechtungen* which never plagued the serene piety of the Silesian reformer. Again, most evangelical theologians would take issue with Schwenckfeld's mystical understanding of faith from a practical and ethical point of view. To be sure, his doctrine is consonant with a concept of salvation as the substantial – if fractional – implantation within the human heart of the Lord's glorified flesh. Faith, then, becomes an emanation of Christ himself. But how is the potential believer to achieve, or better, experience such a supra-rational faith? Schwenckfeld dismisses all means; therefore faith is not something resulting by means of, or amenable to, a psychological-ethical process. Ultimately, then, the gift of faith must come in well-nigh miraculous fashion directly from the Inner Word as part of the Inner Word. In criticizing the ethical deficiencies of the Reformation, Schwenckfeld himself, by substituting a substantial-spiritual concept of a faith which implanted itself supernaturally and impersonally in the waiting subject without the necessary involvement of a rational and religious psychological process, actually propounded a less ethical view of faith and salvation than did other reformers. Having failed to grasp the depths of Luther's concept, Schwenckfeld's own doctrine of faith was hardly a satisfactory substitute, at least by the standards of western theology.

This in theory. In practice, however, as we have had occasion to note, Schwenckfeld was saved from the logical extremes to which his soteriological rationale would lead by a profound ethical sensitivity, and his objections to enthusiasm have already been noted. In this connection Loetscher makes the acute observation: "...whereas in Lutheranism it was the practice that failed to maintain itself on the high level of the evangelical theory, in Schwenckfeld, the defective theory of faith was wisely overruled in practice by a consideration for the religious welfare of the believer." [1]

In conclusion, to characterize Schwenckfeld's place in church history and in the annals of Christian dogma is to note both his indebtedness to the past, as well as his novel combination and repristination of several different but related trends in the chronicles of Christendom. With the Gnostics Schwenckfeld shared a certain tangency in implicitly attaching evil to the creaturely, the material, and the external, although his dualism did not correspond to that of Gnosticism. It more closely resembled that of a baptized Neo-Platonic mysticism which, however, with Augustine, never actually posited the material as non-existence, nor the goal of mystic contemplation as a deifying ecstasy. But like the Christian Neo-Platonist, Origen,

[1] Loetscher, *op. cit.*, 492.

Schwenckfeld interpreted salvation as a liberation from the ruin and punishment of material creaturity. The mode of this redemption was the real, physical process of "God becoming man that we might become divine," typified in Greek-Anatolian theology, and represented in the West particularly by Irenaus, as well as Hilary, Ambrose, and Jerome. In the interests of this mystical, physico-spiritual theory of redemption, Schwenckfeld defended the unity and glory of the person of Christ with all the fervor of Cyril and the Alexandrian school. Much as Bernard of Clairveaux's "Christ-mysticism" was directed to the earthly Jesus, so that of Schwenckfeld was attuned to the heavenly. Lastly, the whole subjective religious interiority of the German mystics – Eckhart, the author of the *Imitatio Christi*, and especially Tauler – also found a sympathetic representation two centuries later in the Silesian reformer who wove many of these strands into his own system.

The theology of Schwenckfeld, however, was no unimaginative restatement of doctrines which had already been elaborated some twelve hundred years earlier. Besides the *nova* of Christ's non-creaturity and the deification of his humanity (which, of course, were approximated in one form or another by some of Schwenckfeld's theological forebears), he was also original in his anthropology, Eucharistic teaching, and his doctrine of the appropriation of salvation through a Christ-implanting, partially Christ-constituting faith. At least among the reformers of his day, Schwenckfeld's definition of faith was unique.

Finally, it was in his concept of the *immediate Erkenntnis Christi* through a physical-hyperphysical, finally mystical gift of faith that Schwenckfeld exposed the foundation of his thought world: the dualism between the material and the spiritual. This dichotomy, which gave structure even to his doctrine of the person and work of Christ, first cast Schwenckfeld in the role of "reformer's reformer" and predisposed him to a theologizing of at least the spiritualist, if not mystical, strain in the history of Christian thought. The shunning of the external and the quest for the internal, then, was Schwenckfeld's lot, his mission, and his glory. For the compendia of church history it may suffice to summarize: Schwenckfeldian theology is centered in the *Erkenntnis Christi*, an immediate, spiritual apprehension and appropriation of the exalted Lord, whose person Schwenckfeld regarded as non-creaturely, whose glorified humanity he equated with divinity, and whose justifying-sanctifying inhabitation was realized through that partial, substantial-spiritual emanation of Christ himself which Schwenckfeld called faith. This is the Schwenckfeldian gospel... all else is commentary.

BIBLIOGRAPHY

For a comprehensive list of the literature concerning Schwenckfeld's life and theology which appeared before 1911, see Karl Ecke, *Schwenckfeld, Luther und der Gedanke einer apostolischen Reformation* (Berlin, 1911), pp. 3-9.

Bibliographies on Schwenckfeld also include:

SCHOTTENLOHER, KARL. *Bibliographie zur deutschen Geschichte im Zeitalter der Glaubensspaltung, 1517-1585*. II. Leipzig, 1935. Pp. 252-60.

WOLF, GUSTAV. *Quellenkunde der deutschen Reformationsgeschichte*. II. Gotha, 1922. Pp. 171-83

A. PRIMARY SOURCES

Corpus Schwenckfeldianorum. Edited by Chester David Hartranft, et al. I-XVII Leipzig, 1907-1939. Volumes I to XV include Schwenckfeld's works from 1521 to 1557 Volume XVI, in MS., contains his writings from 1558 to 1561 The final volume, XVII, also in MS., comprises miscellaneous documents throughout the span of Schwenckfeld's literary activity which were not included in I to XVI. Volumes XVI and XVII are in the process of publication.

Previous to the above, the only attempted larger edition of Schwenckfeld's writings comprised the following four volumes·

Der Erste Theil Der Christlichen Orthodoxischen Bucher und schrifften/ des Edlen/ theuren/ von Gott hoch begnadeten und gottseligen Hans/ Caspar Schwenckfeldt vom hauss Ossing/ Welche vom XXIIII. Jar an/ biss auff das LXII... beschrieben. M.D LXIIII.

Epistolar/ Des Edlen, von Gott hochbegnadete theuwren Mans Caspar Schwenckfeldts von Ossing/ seliger gedachtnis Christliche Lehrhaffte Missiuen oder Sendbrieff/ die er in zeit seines Lebens/ vom XXV. Jare an biss auff das LV .. geschrieben Der Erste Theil. 1566

Epistolar/ Des Edlen, von Gott hochbegnadete Herren Caspar Schwenckfelds von Ossing auss der Schlesien seliger gedechtnus/ Christliche leerhaffte Sendbrieffe und schrifften/ ...von der Bapstischen Leere vnd Glauben/ die er in Zeit seines lebens/ vom XXV Jare an/ biss auff das LXI... geschrieben/ Der Ander Theil in vier Bucher underscheiden. 1570

Das zweite Buch des andern Theils des Epistolars. Darinn Herren Caspar Schwenckfeldts Sendbrieffe begriffen/ die er auff der Lutherischen glauben/ Leere/ Sacrament und Kirchen/ zum theil an Lutherische zum theil sonst an guthertzige Personen geschrieben. M D. LXX.

* * *

Corpus Reformatorum Edited by K. G Bretschneider, *et al* Berlin and Leipzig, 1834 ff

D. Martin Luthers Werke. Kritische Gesamtausgabe Weimar, 1883 ff.

Luthers Sammtliche Werke. Erlangen, 1830 ff.

Patrologiae cursus completus, Series graeca. Edited by J P. Migne, *et al.* Paris, 1857 ff.

Patrologiae cursus completus, Series latina. Edited by J P. Migne, *et al.* Paris, 1844 ff.

B. SECONDARY WORKS

Following are only those writings which have specific reference to Schwenckfeld. Other literature is documented in the text

ALTHAUS, PAUL. *Zur Charakteristic der evangelischen Gebetsliteratur im Reformationsjahrhundert.* Leipzig, 1914.

ANDERS, EDUARD *Geschichte der evangelischen Kirche Schlesiens.* Breslau, 1883

ARNOLD, C. FRANKLIN "Zur Geschichte und Literatur der Schwenckfelder." *Zeitschrift des Vereins fur Geschichte Schlesiens.* Bd. 43. XI. Breslau, 1909. Pp. 291-303.

ARNOLD, GOTTFRIED. *Unpartheyische Kirchen- und Ketzerhistorien* Bd. I. Th. II. Buch XVI. Schaffhausen, 1740. Pp. 1246-99.

BARCLAY, ROBERT. *The Inner Life of the Religious Societies of the Commonwealth.* London, MDCCCLXXVI. Pp. 221-52.

BAUR, FERDINAND CHRISTIAN. *Die christliche Lehre von der Versohnung in ihrer geschichtlichen Entwicklung* Tubingen, 1838. Pp. 459-63.

— *Die christliche Lehre von der Dreieinigkeit und Menschwerdung Gottes in ihrer geschichtlichen Entwicklung.* Tubingen, 1841-43. Pp. 219-56.

— "Zur Geschichte der protestantischen Mystik" *Theologische Jahrbucher.* VII. Tubingen, 1848. Pp 502-28.

BEARD, CHARLES. *The Reformation of the Sixteenth Century in its Relation to Modern Thought and Knowledge* (The Hibbert Lectures). London, 1883. Pp. 212-16.

BERGSTEN, TORSTEN. "Pilgram Marbeck und seine Auseinandersetzung mit Caspar Schwenckfeld." *Kyrkohistorisk Årsskrift* 1957-58. Uppsala, 1958. Pp. 39-135

BORNGRABER, OTTO. *Das Erwachen der philosophischen Spekulation der Reformationszeit.* (Diss., Erlangen). Schwarzenberg i. Sa., 1908.

BORNKAMM, HEINRICH. "Ausserer und innerer Mensch bei Luther und den Spiritualisten " *Imago Dei:* Beiträge zur theologischen Anthropologie. Giessen, 1932 Pp. 85-109.

— "Mystik, Spiritualismus und die Anfänge des Pietismus im Luthertum." *Vortrage der theologischen Konferenz.* Folge 44. Giessen, 1926.

DOLLINGER, J. *Die Reformation, ihre innere Entwicklung und ihre Wirkungen im Umfange des Lutherischen Bekenntnisses.* Bd. I. Regensburg, 1848. Pp. 236-88

DORNER, J. A. *Entwicklungsgeschichte der Lehre von der Person Christi.* Zweiter Theil Berlin, 1853. Pp. 624-36.

— *Geschichte der protestantischen Theologie, besonders in Deutschland.* München, 1867 Pp. 176-82.

EBERLEIN, PAUL GERHARD "Schwenckfelds Urteil uber die Augsburger Konfession." *Jahrbuch fur Schlesische Kirche und Kirchengeschichte* Band 34. Dusseldorf, 1955. Pp. 60-68.

ECKE, KARL. *Das Ratsel der Taufe* Gutersloh, 1952. Pp. 21 ff.

— "Kaspar Schwenckfeld Ungeloste Geistesfragen der Reformationszeit" *Alte und Neue Wege zur lebendigen Gemeinde.* Heft 1 Gutersloh, 1952.

— *Schwenckfeld, Luther und der Gedanke einer apostolischen Reformation* Berlin, 1911

ENDRISS, JULIUS. *Kaspar Schwenckfelds Ulmer Kämpfe* Ulm, 1936

ERBKAM, H. W. *Geschichte der protestantischen Sekten im Zeitalter der Reformation.* Hamburg und Gotha, 1848. Pp. 357-475.

— "Schwenckfeld." *Realencyklopadie fur protestantische Theologie und Kirche.* Zweite Auflage. XIII, pp 776 ff.

ERDMANN, D. "Schwenckfeld" *Allgemeine Deutsche Biographie* XXXIII Leipzig, 1891 Pp 403-12.

Erlauterung fur Herrn Caspar Schwenckfeld, und die Zugethanen seiner Lehre. Sumnytaun, Pa., 1830.

FRENCH, JAMES LESLIE. *The Correspondence of Caspar Schwenckfeld of Ossig and the Landgrave Philip of Hesse, 1535-1561.* Leipzig, 1908.

GERBERT, CAMILL *Geschichte der Strassburger Sectenbewegung zur Zeit der Reformation, 1524-1534* Strassburg, 1889. Pp. 132-41

GRUNHAGEN, E. *Geschichte Schlesiens* II Gotha, 1886.

GRUTZMACHER, RICHARD H. "Schwenckfeld." *Realencyklopadie fur protestantische Theologie und Kirche* Dritte Auflage. XVIII (1906), pp 72-81; and XXIV (1913), pp 482 f.

— *Wort und Geist, Eine historische und dogmatische Untersuchung zum Gnadenmittel des Wortes.* Leipzig, 1902 Pp 158-73.

HAGEN, KARL. *Deutschlands literarische und religiose Verhaltnisse im Reformationszeitalter* III. Erlangen, 1841. Pp. 237-40

HAHN, GEORGIUS LUDOVICUS *Schwenckfeldii Sententia de Christi Persona et Opere Exposita. Commentatio Historico-Theologica* Vratislaviae, MDCCCXLVII

HAMPE, O. *Zur Biographie Kaspars von Schwenckfeld* Jauer, 1882.

HEGLER, ALFRED. "Beitrage zur Geschichte der Mystik in der Reformationszeit" *Archiv fur Reformationsgeschichte.* Erganzungsband I. Berlin, 1906

— *Geist und Schrift bei Sebastian Franck. Eine Studie zur Geschichte des Spiritualismus in der Reformationszeit* Freiburg i B , 1892.

HEYD, A "Blaurer. Schnepf. Schwenckfeld. Ein Bruchstuck aus dem ersten Capitel der Reformationsgeschichte Wurtembergs" *Tubinger Zeitschrift für Theologie* Heft IV. Tubingen, 1838 Pp 1-48.

HIRSCH, EMANUEL "Zum Verstandnis Schwenckfelds." *Festgabe von Fachgenossen und Freunden Karl Müller.* Tubingen, 1922 Pp. 145-70.

Historische Nachricht Von dem Vor zweyhundert Jahren beruhmten und verruffenen Schlesischen Edelmann, HERRN Caspar Schwenckfeld von Ossing, Samt beygefugter Anzahl seiner Schrifften. Prentzlau, 1744.

HOFFMANN, FRANZ *Caspar Schwenckfelds Leben und Lehren* Erster Teil. Berlin, 1897.

JONES, RUFUS M. *Spiritual Reformers in the Sixteenth and Seventeenth Centuries.* London, 1914 Pp. 64-87.

KADELBACH, OSWALD. *Ausfuhrliche Geschichte Kaspar v. Schwenckfelds und der Schwenkfelder in Schlesien, der Ober-Lausitz und Amerika, nebst ihren Glaubensschriften von 1524-1860.* Lauban, 1860

KLUGE, A. "Caspar von Schwenckfelds Stellung zu Theologie und Kirche." *Correspondenzblatt des Vereins für Geschichte der evangelischen Kirche Schlesiens.* XVI (1918). Pp. 7-29.

— "Leben und Entwicklungsgang Schwenckfelds" *Correspondenzblatt, etc.* XV (1917). Pp. 220-44.

KOHLER, WALTHER. "Kaspar Schwenckfeld." *Die Religion in Geschichte und Gegenwart.* Zweite Auflage. V (1931) pp. 354 f.

— Critique of Ecke in *Theologische Literaturzeitung.* VII (1913) pp. 209 ff.

KOYRÉ, ALEXANDRE. *Mystiques, Spirituels, Alchimistes du XVIe siècle allemand.* Paris, 1955. P. 1 ff.

KRIEBEL, HOWARD WIEGNER *The Schwenckfelders in Pennsylvania.* Lancaster, Pa, 1904.

KUHN, JOHANNES *Toleranz und Offenbarung.* Leipzig, 1923. Pp. 140-56.

LINDEBOOM, J. *Stiefkinderen van het Christendom.* 's-Gravenhage, 1929. Pp. 164-90.

LOESCHER, VALENTIN ERNST. *Dissertatio de Schvengfeldismo in Pietismo renato.* Wittenberger Disputation, XI. Okt. 1708.

LOETSCHER, FREDERICK WILLIAM. "Schwenckfeld's Participation in the Eucharistic Controversy of the Sixteenth Century." *The Princeton Theological Review.* IV. Philadelphia, July and October, 1906. Pp. 352-86; 454-500.

LOHMEYER, ERNST. "Caspar Schwenckfeld von Ossig." *Schlesische Lebensbilder.* IV. Breslau, 1931. Pp. 40-49.

MARON, GOTTFRIED. *Individualismus und Gemeinschaft bei Caspar v. Schwenckfeld. Seine Theologie, dargestellt mit besonderer Ausrichtung auf seinen Kirchenbegriff.* Unpublished dissertation, University of Gottingen, 1956

MARONIER, J. H *Het Inwendig Woord* Amsterdam, 1890. Pp. 51-79.

PIETZ, REINHOLD. *Der Mensch Ohne Christus, Eine Untersuchung zur Anthropologie Caspar Schwenckfelds.* Unpublished dissertation, University of Tubingen, 1956.

PLANCK, G. J. *Geschichte der Entstehung, der Veranderungen und der Bildung unseres protestantischen Lehrbegriffs.* Funften Bandes erster Theil Leipzig, 1798. Pp 75-250.

PREGER, WILHELM. *Matthias Flacius Illyricus und seine Zeit.* Erlangen, 1859. Pp 298-353.

SALIG, CHRISTIAN AUGUST. *Vollstandige Historie der Augspurgischen Confession und derselben Apologie zugethanen Kirchen* Halle, 1730. Pp. 950-1116.

SCHENKEL, DANIEL. *Das Wesen des Protestantismus aus den Quellen des Reformationszeitalters dargestellt.* Schaffhausen, 1862 Pp. 382-87.

SCHLUSSELBURG, CONRAD. "De Stenckfeldistis." *Catalogus haereticorum.* Liber Decimus Francofurti, 1599.

SCHNEIDER, A. F. H. *Ueber den geschichtlichen Verlauf der Reformation in Liegnitz.* Abtheilung I. Berlin, 1860

SCHNEIDER, DANIEL. *Unpartheyische Prufung des Caspar Schwengfelds und Grundliche Vertheydigung der Augspurgischen Confession.* Giessen, 1708

SCHOEPS, HANS JOACHIM. "Vom Himmlischen Fleisch Christi." *Sammlung*

Gemeinverständlicher Vortrage und Schriften aus dem Gebiet der Theologie und Religionsgeschichte. 195/196. Tubingen, 1951. Pp 25-36.

SCHULTZ, CHRISTOPH. *Compendium, das ist kurze Zusammenfassung und Inbegriff der Christlichen Glaubens-Lehren* Philadelphia, 1836.

SCHULTZ, SELINA GERHARD. *Caspar Schwenckfeld von Ossig.* Norristown, Pa., 1947.

SEEBERG, ERICH. "Der Gegensatz zwischen Zwingli, Schwenckfeld, und Luther " *Reinhold-Seeberg-Festschrift.* I. Leipzig, 1929. Pp 43-80.

SEIPT, ALLEN ANDERS *Schwenkfelder Hymnology and The Sources of the First Schwenkfelder Hymn-Book Printed in America.* Philadelphia, 1909.

SIPPELL, THEODOR "Caspar Schwenckfeld " *Die Christliche Welt* Funfundzwanzigster Jahrgang. Marburg i. H , 1911 Pp. 866-71, 897-900; 925-27; 955-57; 963-66.

SOFFNER, JOHANNES. *Geschichte der Reformation in Schlesien* Breslau, 1887.

STAEHELIN, ERNST. "Stimmen radikalerer Reformer." *Die Verkundigung des Reiches Gottes in der Kirche Jesu Christi.* IV. Basel, 1957. Pp. 356-65.

TROELTSCH, ERNST. *Die Soziallehren der christlichen Kirchen und Gruppen.* Tubingen, 1912. Pp. 881-86.

URNER, HANS. "Die Taufe bei Caspar Schwenckfeld." *Theologische Literaturzeitung.* Heft 6 (1948) pp 329-42.

WACH, JOACHIM "Caspar Schwenckfeld, a Pupil and a Teacher in the School of Christ." *The Journal of Religion* XXVI No. 1. January, 1946. Pp. 1-29.

WIGAND, JOHANN. *De Schwengfeldismo. Dogmata et argumenta.* Lipsiae, 1587.

WILLIAMS, GEORGE HUNSTON "Documents Illustrative of the Radical Reformation." *The Library of Christian Classics.* XXV. Philadelphia, 1957. Pp. 161-81.

www.ingramcontent.com/pod-product-compliance
Lightning Source LLC
Chambersburg PA
CBHW050839160426
43192CB00011B/2086